2009 02 20

165101

THE BEATLES'
ABBEY ROAD
MEDLEY

Extended Forms in Popular Music

DATE DUE	RETURNED

JK

SCARECROW PRESS, INC.

Published in the United States of America
by Scarecrow Press, Inc.
A wholly owned subsidary of
The Rowman & Littlefield Publishing Group, Inc.
4501 Forbes Boulevard, Suite 200, Lanham, Maryland 20706
www.scarecrowpress.com

Estover Road
Plymouth PL6 7PY
United Kingdom

British Library Cataloguing in Publication Information Available

Library of Congress Cataloging-in-Publication Data

MacFarlane, Thomas, 1960–
  The Beatles' Abbey Road medley : extended forms in popular music /
Thomas MacFarlane.
     p. cm.
  Includes bibliographical references (p.) and index.
  ISBN-13: 978-0-8108-6019-3 (pbk. : alk. paper)
  ISBN-10: 0-8108-6019-8 (pbk. : alk. paper)
 1. Beatles. Abbey Road. 2. Rock music—1961–1970—Analysis, appreciation.
I. Title.
ML421.B4M155 2008
782.42166092'2—dc22   2007024817

♾™ The paper used in this publication meets the minimum requirements of
American National Standard for Information Sciences—Permanence of Paper
for Printed Library Materials, ANSI/NISO Z39.48-1992.
Manufactured in the United States of America.

This book is dedicated to my parents,
Francis and Jean, and to my son, Graham

CONTENTS

PART III   CONCLUSIONS

ACKNOWLEDGMENTS

I would like to acknowledge the following music scholars, listed in alphabetical order, whose insightful comments greatly contributed to my research: Dr. Cathy Benedict, Prof. Tom Beyer, Prof. Joel Chadabe, Dr. Marc-Antonio Consoli, Dr. Justin Dello Joio, Prof. Tom Doczi, Dr. Stelio Dubbiosi, Dr. Youngmi Ha, Dr. Paul Horan, Dr. Min Kim, Prof. Sonny Kompanek, Dr. Esther Lamneck, Dr. Robert Landy, Dr. Annette LeSiege, Dr. Panayotis Mavromatis, Dr. Catherine Moore, Dr. Edward Raditz, Dr. Steven Rosenhaus, Dr. Adelaida Reyes Schramm, Dr. David Schroeder, Dr. Philip Tagg, and Dr. Grant Wenaus.

The following friends and collaborators must also be acknowledged for their varied and astute observations regarding the Beatles' distinctive approach to music composition: Buddy Baker, Frank Balesteri, Joe Bank, Rebecca Birmingham, Dom Buccafusco, Clem Burke, Willie Byrd, James Paul Christie, Bob Dokus, Abel Dominguez, Mike Grau, Cornelius Hearn, Sal Iannaci, Frank Infante, Harry Kopy, Gregg Leto, Dominick Maita, Arthur Marino, R. Stevie Moore, Giro Mosca, Don Neumuller, Mark Paradine, Diana Pardo, Bob Sanders, Tom Sullivan, Dan Veksler, and Peter Zervoulis. I offer a special note of thanks to Mr. Peter Brown for graciously consenting to a personal interview, conducted in New York City on August 5, 2003.

I would also like to express my appreciation to Dr. David Elliott, Dr. Robert Rowe, and Dr. Gage Averill for their generosity and patience during the research that went into the preparation of this book. In addition, I am indebted to Dr. John Gilbert, Dr. Dinu Ghezzo, and Dr. Kenneth Peacock, whose insights and guidance kept me on track from the earliest stages of my research. Thanks also to Dr. Ron Sadoff for his sound advice and endless good will. Finally, I especially wish to thank Dr. Lawrence Ferrara, not only for his constant support and encouragement, but also for the eclectic method of analysis that has given this writer new ears to hear and new eyes to see.

•   •   •

The author and publisher gratefully acknowledge permission to use the following lyrics: "Because"; "You Never Give Me Your Money"; "Sun King"; "Mean Mr. Mustard"; "Polythene Pam"; "She Came in Through the Bathroom Window"; "Carry That Weight"; "Golden Slumbers"; "The End"; "Her Majesty." Words and Music by John Lennon and Paul McCartney. Copyright © 1969 by Sony/ATV Songs LLC. Copyright Renewed. All Rights Administered by Sony/ATV Music Publishing, 8 Music Square West, Nashville, TN 37203. International Copyright Secured All Rights Reserved.

Rhapsody in Blue by George Gershwin, copyright © 1924 (Renewed) WB Music Corp. Gershwin and George Gershwin are registered trademarks of Gershwin Enterprises. *Rhapsody in Blue* is a trademark of the George Gershwin Family Trust. All Rights Reserved including Public Performance. Reprinted with Permission of Alfred Publishing Co., Inc.

In-person interview with Peter Brown (August 5, 2003), speech, recordings, and transcribed text. Used by Permission.

All photographs provided by Photofest, 32 East 31st Street, 5th floor, New York, NY 10016. Used by Permission.

EXAMPLES

Part I

CONTEXT

1

A BEGINNING

In September 1969 the Beatles released *Abbey Road*, an album that employs a wide variety of progressive musical ideas firmly rooted in the group's meticulous approach to multitrack recording. Rising to the high standards set by their previous work, *Abbey Road* presents a series of tracks that constitute a significant high point in the group's overall musical corpus. Of particular interest is a concluding sequence of seemingly unrelated fragments woven together in a musical form that has thus far defied all attempts at facile classification. The purpose of this book is to present an analysis of these fragments (commonly known as the *Abbey Road* medley) in order to understand and explain the emergent musical form and to thereby clarify the relationships that exist between music recording and music composition.

GETTING BETTER

In recent decades, an appreciation of the Beatles has been growing steadily as each new generation discovers and explores the emotional richness and technical complexity of the group's music. At the same time, there is an emerging academic scholarship that stresses its importance to twentieth-century musical development. The nature of this scholarship has run the gamut from traditional formal analysis to progressive philosophical discourse.

On the one hand analysts whose views are firmly rooted in the formalist tradition have sought to validate Beatles music by stressing its clear correlation with masterworks of the Western musical canon. In *The Beatles: A Musical Evolution* author Terence J. O'Grady points out that:

> While Lennon's love ballad "Because" is not, as he suggests, Beethoven's "Moonlight Sonata" (Op. 27, No. 2 in C# minor) played backwards, the song does resemble the first movement of Beethoven's work in some harmonic aspects (especially the use of the Neapolitan or flat-II chord), its arpeggiated texture, and some aspects of the melodic rhythm.[1]

Meanwhile, critiques by writers like Ed Whitley have taken a decidedly nontraditional approach to late-period Beatles music (1967–1969). In his essay "The Postmodern *White Album* (2000)" Whitley asserts the presence of postmodern aesthetic processes within that album's widely divergent and often baffling song sequence: "By employing the disruptive aesthetics of postmodern art, the *White Album* calls attention away from itself as a source of meaning and instead clears a space where readers can engage the issues of what popular music is and what role it plays."[2]

Judging from these diverse yet valid analyses, and others, it seems clear that analysis of the Beatles' music has now achieved a high degree of credibility within the academic community. It is in the spirit of that achievement that this study of the *Abbey Road* medley is offered.

MEDLEYS AND EXTENDED FORMS

Although the Beatles themselves offered no clear designation in the album's liner notes, the work in question has come to be known as the *Abbey Road* medley.[3] But what exactly is a medley? *The New Grove Dictionary of Music and Musicians* defines a medley as

> a succession of well-known tunes strung together, generally without any formal construction. . . . A medley is similar to a potpourri, though generally of a smoother construction. The constituent tunes are very often from

a similar source, as for example "a medley of tunes from X" or "a medley of songs by Y."[4]

On the basis of a preliminary analysis, the *Abbey Road* medley does not correspond to *Grove*'s definition. Although the various song fragments are listed as discrete tracks in the album's liner notes, one can readily detect musical elements that suggest a preponderance of organic unity—for example, chromatic mediant relationships that suggest structural implications, the restatement of themes that suggest the presence of developmental processes, and an economy of means with regard to the reworking of harmonic, melodic, and rhythmic material. Taken together, these elements challenge the notion that the work in question corresponds to Grove's definition of the term *medley*. It therefore seems that the *Abbey Road* medley is not a *medley* at all; rather, it is an extended form in three movements.

Extended form corresponds to the term *cyclic form*, which *Grove* defines as

> Music in which a later movement reintroduces thematic material of an earlier movement. . . . Beethoven (*An die ferne Geliebte*, Piano Sonata in A op.101), Schubert (Piano Trio in Eb; Fantasie in C for violin and piano), and Berlioz (*Symphonie fantastique*) laid the foundations on which Mendelssohn, Schumann, Liszt, and Franck elevated cyclic principles to great importance, associated with the widespread application of thematic transformation and the desire for greater continuity between separate movements, all methods of establishing a tighter cohesion in multi-movement forms. Since, the nineteenth-century cyclic form has been adopted as a regular stock-in-trade of musical structure.[5]

The organic elements evident in a preliminary analysis tend to correspond to *Grove*'s definition of *cyclic form* and thus suggest the presence of a complex organizational structure at work within the *Abbey Road* medley.

In order to facilitate the analysis that will be undertaken in part 2 (chapters 4–8) of this study, the following structural model is proposed:

Prelude
  "Because"

Movement I
   "You Never Give Me Your Money"
   "Out of College/That Magic Feeling"
   "One Sweet Dream"
Movement II
   "Sun King/Mean Mr. Mustard"
   "Polythene Pam/She Came in Through the Bathroom Window"
Movement III
   "Golden Slumbers/Carry That Weight"
   "The End"
Postlude
   "Her Majesty"

The creation of this model is predicated on the presence of directed tonal motion toward structural goals, as well as various thematic threads evident in the text. The use of the terms *prelude* and *postlude* in reference to the tracks "Because" and "Her Majesty" is intended to foreground the role that each of these songs plays in bracketing the inner movements. The term *movement* is used in reference to the three large sections that constitute the main body of the work and is not intended to imply any overt connections with the traditions of Western musical practice, as in Haydn's String Quartets, Op. 33; Beethoven's Symphony # 5, Op. 67; or Berlioz's Symphony Fantastique, Op. 14.[6]

COMPOSING TO TAPE

In the twentieth century, the advent of recording technologies granted the music listener unprecedented access to the inner workings of the compositional process. Alternate takes of the kind featured in the Beatles' *Anthology* CD allow one the opportunity to hear how recorded works evolve over successive tracking and overdubbing sessions. These recordings are similar in function to the preliminary sketches employed by classical composers—and in many ways constitute the true "score" of a musical work.

   In his essay "The Beatles as Composers: The Genesis of *Abbey Road*, Side Two" Walter Everett observed that the recording method typically employed by the late-period Beatles (three or four instruments plus reference vocal as the basic track) resembles "Mozart's habit of writing a *particella* draft for an opera or concerto: the structural solo and bass lines would often be committed to paper first, after which time the inner parts would be composed and assigned instrumentation."[7] On that basis, recorded works can be seen to function simultaneously as art objects and important documents of the creative process.

At this point, it is reasonable to assert that the *Abbey Road* medley is the culmination of the Beatles' late-period (1967–1969) experimentation with musical form. However, in order to accurately describe the significance of this work, we must also consider the ways in which the medium of sound recording has fundamentally affected the compositional process. Toward that end, we may posit an historical line of demarcation created by the appearance of *Poeme Electronique*, an electro-acoustic composition conceived and realized entirely on magnetic tape by Edgard Varese for the Brussels World's Fair in 1958.[8]

In addition to its considerable aesthetic and historical significance, *Poeme Electronique* delineated a shift in the functional definition of sound recording from archival documentation to what might be described as a reification of the musical canvas. As a result of this shift, the sound space previously associated with theaters and concert halls had now become a conceptual space that the contemporary composer could engage as a medium upon which to paint musical sound. The level at which the Beatles engaged this new canvas suggests that they should not only be regarded as the creators of their musical compositions but also as the authors of their recorded works.

AUTHORSHIP OF THE RECORDED WORK

In his 1954 article, director Francois Truffaut outlined the theory of the *auteur*. In essence, this critical view asserts that it is the director who must ultimately be regarded as the true author of a film, since it is his or her vision that dominates the entire creative process.[9] It was Truffaut's belief that, despite the collaboration necessary for the creation of any cinematic work, it is the director who is ultimately responsible for what is presented on the screen.

In a similar manner, an increasing number of composers in the mid-
to late twentieth century began engaging the recording medium not
merely as the means for recreating live performances but also as an essential element in the compositional process. Virgil Moorefield discussed this shift by focusing on composer-producer Brian Eno's distinctive approach to recorded sound:

> His approach to the studio as a full-fledged musical instrument was
> groundbreaking, and beginning in the mid-seventies his numerous inter-
> views featured discussions of pop music in terms that were altogether new.
> A fan of "roots" rock as well as reggae, he pointed out the implications of
> the techniques employed in the modern recording studio and traced his
> own conceptual lineage as a composer back through Steve Reich and John
> Cage to Erik Satie.[10]

Eno's reference to a conceptual lineage with composers Steve Reich,
John Cage, and Erik Satie underscores the parallels that exist between
sound recording and music composition.[11] These connections to a more
serious musical tradition can also be found in the work of the Beatles. In
their case, however, the links were not only conceptual; they were also
very concrete and due primarily to the influence of EMI staff producer
George Martin.

SIR GEORGE MARTIN

Sir George Martin is commonly considered to be the Beatles' most important link with the musical traditions of the past. An accomplished in-
strumentalist and arranger educated at London's Guildhall School of
Music, Martin's skills were essential to attaining the professional luster
that became an indispensable element in the Beatles' music.[12] But in addition to his vast contribution to their compositions, Martin was also responsible for the technical innovations that characterized many late-
period (1967–1969) Beatles recordings. Working with engineer Geoff
Emerick, Martin was able to turn EMI Studios into a virtual laboratory
of recorded sound.[13]

This fact suggests a possible connection between the spirit of experimentation that characterized EMI Studios during the 1960s and similar developments that were taking place at the Cologne Studio and Radio France. One wonders if Martin and the EMI staff were familiar with the seminal work of recording pioneers like Pierre Schaeffer and Edgard Varese. As it turns out, they were not only aware of these developments, but Martin himself had direct experience with the creation of electro-acoustic music, albeit with a relatively obscure and rather amusing pseudonym—Ray Cathode.

As Martin himself recalled: "Creating atmosphere and sound pictures, . . . that was my bag. I did a lot of it before the Beatles even came along. In 1962, Parlophone issued a single called 'Time Beat/Waltz in Orbit,' a compilation of electronic sounds, composed by a certain 'Ray Cathode'—me."[14] In *The Unknown Paul McCartney: McCartney and the Avant-garde*, author Ian Peel describes how this obscure recording "mixed live musicians over a purely synthesized electronic rhythm track Martin had created with the Radiophonic Workshop."[15] The workshop described was an in-house unit created by the BBC to supply sound and music effects for the various radio and television programs in its schedule.[16] Through the work of researchers Daphne Oram, Delia Derbyshire, and Desmond Briscoe, the BBC Radiophonic Workshop carried on, albeit within a commercial context, the kind of avant-garde experimentation that was a key feature of the work done at the Cologne Studio and Radio France.[17]

George Martin's experience with both traditional and progressive approaches to music composition thus explains his critical role in the Beatles' creative process. He clearly provided continuity with the musical traditions of the past, but he was also a viable link to contemporary music, which was becoming increasingly dependent on recording technology as the means for its realization.

PET SOUNDS

The most significant antecedent in popular music for the formal development that characterized the Beatles' late period (1967–1969) can be found in the work of one of the most successful musical groups of the 1960s, the Beach Boys. Between 1961 and 1965, the Beach Boys produced a series of singles and LPs that exhibited an increasingly expansive level of musical sophistication. The architect of this group's sound was composer Brian Wilson, whose attempts to blend the jazz-based vocal harmonies of the Four Freshmen with the energetic sounds of southern California "surf" music resulted in a highly distinctive and original musical style.[18]

In addition to his melodic and harmonic experimentation, Wilson was also intrigued by the aesthetic possibilities of sound recording. Virgil Moorefield describes how Wilson sought to build on the innovations of the legendary producer Phil Spector: "Wilson admired the work of Phil Spector and made it his business to emulate his production techniques, to the point of working with Spector's hand-picked group of session musicians, the Wrecking Crew, in the same studio (L.A.'s now defunct Gold Star Studios), and with the same engineer (Larry Levine)."[19]

Following Phil Spector's example, and motivated by a perceived musical rivalry with the Beatles, Wilson produced *Pet Sounds*, an album which has consistently garnered high critical praise for its innovative approach to arrangement and production. Several months later came *Good Vibrations,* a single that expanded the formal development of *Pet Sounds* by means of an elaborate series of tape edits that juxtaposed contrasting musical tempos and textures in a dazzling mosaic of recorded sound.[20] As Moorefield points out:

> "Good Vibrations" is a clear example of the use of the studio as a compositional device. The fact that it is so clearly contrived, that its seams show so obviously, does not detract from its appeal as a song in the least. Listening to "Good Vibrations" today, it is patently obvious that it is spliced together from recordings made in different spaces. Yet the music is powerful, a heady mix of exceptionally polished vocal harmonies and experimental instrumentation.[21]

Regrettably, Wilson's efforts to build on the success of both *Pet Sounds* and *Good Vibrations* were abandoned in 1967 due to personal problems brought on by excessive drug use.[22] However, the significance of his achievements did not go unnoticed. In the book *Many Years from*

Now, biographer Barry Miles writes that "Paul [McCartney] regarded *Pet Sounds* as one of the greatest popular-music albums ever made and was effusive in its praise, particularly for the way in which it proved that the bass player need not play the root note of a chord but can weave a melody around it of its own. He recommended the album to everyone he met."[23]

Impressed by Wilson's achievements, McCartney was determined that the Beatles' next release should expand the focus of their work to include a variety of sounds and textures not normally associated with popular music. The resulting album, *Sgt. Pepper's Lonely Hearts Club Band* (1967), is remarkably varied in both artistic conception and technical execution. In particular, the album's final track, "A Day in the Life," represents a highly innovative use of recording technique and is arguably the Beatles' first attempt to push song-form into the realm of the symphonic. Although the entire album does not exhibit the level of musical sophistication the Beatles would achieve toward the end of their career, it does build significantly on *Pet Sounds*—and thus paves the way for the formal and technical experimentation that would characterize the *Abbey Road* medley.

NOTES

1. Terence J. O'Grady, *The Beatles: A Musical Evolution* (Boston: Twayne Publishers, 1983), 161.

2. Ian Inglis, ed., *The Beatles, Popular Music, and Society: A Thousand Voices* (New York: St. Martin's Press, 2000), 122.

3. Mark Lewisohn, *The Beatles' Recording Sessions* (New York: Harmony Books, 1988), 176.

4. Stanley Sadie, ed., *The New Grove Dictionary of Music and Musicians, Second Edition, Volume Sixteen* (New York: Thames & Hudson, 2001), 269.

5. Sadie, ed., *New Grove Dictionary, Volume Six,* 797–98.

6. In earlier drafts, a conscious effort was made to avoid the use of the term *movement* for the reasons given in the text. However, each attempt at supplying an alternate term for these sections, in addition to unduly complicating the formal analysis, seemed to imply the term to the reader anyway. It was therefore decided to use the term *movement* in an effort to avoid the ambiguities that might arise from any efforts to avoid it.

7. Walter Everett, "The Beatles as Composers: The Genesis of *Abbey Road*, Side Two," in *Concert Music, Rock, and Jazz since 1945: Essays and Analytical Studies*, ed. Elizabeth West Marvin and Richard Hermann, 172–228 (Rochester, NY: University of Rochester Press, 1995).

8. Peter Manning, *Electronic and Computer Music* (New York: Oxford University Press, 2004), 82.

9. James Monaco, *How to Read a Film: The World of Movies, Media, and Multimedia, Language, History, Theory* (New York: Oxford University Press, 2000), 410.

10. Virgil Edwin Moorefield, "From the Illusion of Reality to the Reality of Illusion: The Changing Role of the Producer in the Pop Recording Studio" (PhD diss., Princeton University, 2001), 72–73. Moorefield has since adapted his dissertation into a fascinating book, *The Producer as Composer: Shaping the Sounds of Popular Music* (Cambridge, MA: MIT Press, 2005).

11. On a related note, Paul McCartney has been forthcoming regarding his fondness for composers like Steve Reich, and he seemed in his early solo work to be familiar with Reich's essay, "Music as a Gradual Process." On his first solo release, *McCartney* (1970), he included an excerpt of "Glasses," a fascinating piece in which he and his wife Linda played a collection of wine glasses that were filled with varying amounts of water. Since a composition of this kind has the potential to unfold continuously, it resonates with Reich's observation that, "once the process is set up and loaded it runs by itself." Ian Peel, *The Unknown Paul McCartney: McCartney and the Avant-garde* (London and Richmond, Surrey: Reynolds & Hearn, 2002), 71–72.

12. Sadie, ed., *The New Grove Dictionary, Volume Fifteen*, 912.

13. Lewisohn, *Recording Sessions*, 79.

14. George Martin and William Pearson, *Summer of Love: The Making of Sgt. Pepper* (London: Macmillan, 1994), 83.

15. Peel, *The Unknown Paul McCartney*, 22.

16. Peel, *The Unknown Paul McCartney*, 22–23.

17. Manning, *Electronic and Computer Music*, 72–73.

18. Sadie, ed., *New Grove Dictionary, Volume Three*, 17–18.

19. Moorefield, "From the Illusion of Reality to the Reality of Illusion," 28.

20. At the conclusion of a discussion of the Beach Boys' experimental style, author Daniel Harrison presents a persuasive argument that the group's mid-1960s output, although influential, must ultimately be viewed as a failure, since it is too experimental for the average listener and not experimental enough for the avant-garde. However, one could also argue that *Pet Sounds* and the unfinished *Smile* album might be better understood within the context of minimalism. The completed songs and song fragments from this pe-

riod exhibit many of the defining elements of minimalism and also seem to create the suspension of temporal perception typical of works that employ phasing techniques. If this is the case, then *Pet Sounds* and *Smile* may yet find their proper place in the history of twentieth-century music as an early example of what might be described as *minimalist pop*. [Daniel Harrison, "After Sundown: The Beach Boys' Experimental Music" in *Understanding Rock: Essays in Musical Analysis*, ed. John Covach and Graeme M. Boone (New York: Oxford University Press, 1997), 33–57.]

21. Moorefield, "From the Illusion of Reality to the Reality of Illusion," 32–33.

22. Sadie, ed., *New Grove Dictionary, Volume Three*, 17–18.

23. Barry Miles and Paul McCartney, *Many Years from Now* (New York: H. Holt, 1997), 281.

2

IT'S BEEN A
LONG, LONG, LONG TIME

On approaching the Beatles' work, one can be easily overwhelmed by the sheer variety of the band's artistic output. Clearly, they were composers, performers, and recording artists—but they were also film stars (*A Hard Day's Night*; *Help!*), directors (*Magical Mystery Tour*), authors (John Lennon's *In His Own Write*; *A Spaniard in the Works*), and radio comics (*The Beatles' Christmas Album*[1]). The diverse nature of this material suggests an intuitive awareness of the aesthetic potential of mass communication, which manifested itself in the group's ability to project a collective personality to the public. In retrospect, they seem now to have been heralding the arrival of a new kind of celebrity, one that was seemingly natural yet thoroughly acclimated to the various media, which they actively engaged in the creation of their art.

IT'S ALL TOO MUCH

The Beatles' ability to access the growing potential of mass media is evident in their first performance at New York's Shea Stadium on August 23, 1965. On that date, more than fifty-five thousand people attended what was essentially a "happening."[2] Like many of the group's concerts between 1963 and 1966, the most audible element here was not the music; rather, it was the near-continuous screams of fans mesmerized by the presence of a band they had only experienced through records and films. In a very real sense, as this prime example shows, it is the audience, not the group, that creates the event.

Viewing the footage of this concert with the benefit of hindsight, one is struck by the seeming innocence of the Beatles themselves.[3] Perched on a makeshift stage in the middle of a baseball diamond, they laugh and joke their way through a thirty-minute set that had, by that time, become routine. They certainly seem delighted but also perplexed by the wild hysteria going on all around them.

In an interview from the Beatles' *Anthology*, George Harrison described the group's perceptions from the eye of the storm by pointing out that "It was nice to be popular, but when you saw the size of it, it was ridiculous, and it felt dangerous because everybody was out of hand and out of line. . . . They were all caught up in the mania. It was as if they were all in a big movie and we were the ones trapped in the middle of it. It was a very strange feeling."[4] Harrison's comments suggest that the Beatles were not truly in control of the phenomenon of their own success. Despite their remarkable ability to project themselves through the media, evidence suggests that they were as surprised as anyone by how great their fame had grown.

ALL TOGETHER ON THE WIRELESS MACHINE

The appearance of unaffectedness that was evident onstage at Shea was an important aspect of the Beatles' early appeal. Curiously, their tendency to "put on an act" when confronted by the spectacle of their own success only served to heighten their apparent lack of pretension. During impromptu interviews, the group members always seemed acutely aware that the camera or microphone was there, yet somehow they managed to appear guileless and genuine in their responses.

The following comments, based on actual Beatles press conferences and recreated in the film *A Hard Day's Night* (1964) illustrate the band's peculiar media savvy:

REPORTER: Tell me, how did you find America?

JOHN LENNON: Turn left at Greenland.

REPORTER: Has success changed your life?

GEORGE HARRISON: Yes.

REPORTER: What would you call that hairstyle you're wearing?

GEORGE HARRISON: Arthur.[5]

The cheeky wit evident in this dialogue is also on display in *The Beatles' Christmas Album*, a compilation of original recordings released yearly to the group's fan club from 1963 through 1969.[6] Although the early records in this series are of a fairly routine nature, the group soon abandoned the industry practice of recording simple holiday greetings for their fans and embarked instead on a series of absurdist comedy sketches, which were augmented by song parodies of remarkable sophistication. In retrospect, these recordings seem to suggest the influence of the popular British radio series *The Goon Show*. Consider the following exchange from the 1967 record titled *Christmas Time Is Here Again*:

NIGEL: Sitting with me in the studio tonight is a cross-section of British youth. I'd like first of all to speak to you, Sir Gerald.

SIR GERALD: Oh, not a bit of it. We had a job to do, Nigel.

NIGEL: Ah, yes, yes, quite. I don't think you're answering my question.

SIR GERALD: Oh, let me put it this way—there was a job to be done.

SINGERS: Christmas time is here again! Christmas time is here again!

ANNOUNCER: On to the next round! Bingo! Bingo! Ha! Ha![7]

In a biography of Peter Sellers titled *Mr. Strangelove*, author Ed Sikov described how *The Goon Show* (1951–1960) evolved as "a series of bizarre sketches broken up by musical interludes. The comedians [Peter Sellers, Spike Milligan, Harry Secombe, and Michael Bentine] would do funny voices, make funny noises, and generally act strange, and then a jazz band would come on."[8] This sounds remarkably similar to the tone of *The Beatles' Christmas Album*, as well as some of the group's more whimsical songs, such as *You Know My Name (Look Up the Number)*, *Yellow Submarine*, and *All Together Now*.

Like the Goons, the Beatles seemed to view language not merely as an agency of meaning but also as a game whose purpose was to point out the seemingly irreducible nature of human experience. This canny attitude toward life and language can be traced directly back to the group's humble origins in Liverpool, England.

BENEATH THE BLUE SUBURBAN SKIES

The Beatles began their musical career in Liverpool in the late 1950s. Although an important seaport in the early part of the twentieth century, the city had fallen on hard times following the end of World War II. In an interview conducted on August 5, 2003, with author and Beatles confidante Peter Brown, the conversation touched on the distinctive resilience of the Liverpool character that originated in an atmosphere of increasing economic hardship:

> It was an amazingly successful English port. As the twentieth century went on, it became less and less so. And in our day, in the 1950s and 1960s it was struggling a bit. But there was always an arrogance about the working class Liverpudlians like, "Fuck you," you know, "we'll manage on our own." And it was like the old story that a lot of comedians came from Liverpool, but you had to be a comedian to come from Liverpool. So there was always an attitude about Liverpudlians, and I think that The Beatles, because they came from that culture . . . learned to be very independent and that attitude became their thing.[9]

In addition to nurturing an innate toughness in the adolescent Beatles, Liverpool also provided an ideal environment for fostering the group's rapidly expanding musical acumen. In the same interview, Brown commented on the unique access that Liverpool musicians had to music from divergent cultural sources:

> Also, the other thing about Liverpool was the fact that there was a lot of knowledge about American music that wasn't available in the rest of the

country because of the sailors. A lot of the young, working-class boys
would go to sea initially. They would start going into the Merchant
Marines when they were sixteen, seventeen, eighteen years old. And
they would go to sea to make some money. And, of course, a lot of those
would go to America, and they would spend time in America, they would
buy American records, because in those days, of course, the radio in
Britain was very restrictive, and there wasn't much going on. So we in
Liverpool, and in the record stores that Brian [Epstein] and I worked in,
were much more sophisticated about American music than probably the
rest of the country.[10]

As a result of the availability that Brown describes, Liverpool musicians
would regularly learn American songs by rote and incorporate them directly into their stage acts.[11] Over time, this process of assimilation resulted in the development of a highly original musical style that came to
be known as Merseybeat.

In an article from *The New Grove Dictionary of Music and Musicians*, Allan F. Moore describes the essential elements of the Mersey
Sound:

In Liverpool, Merseybeat was spearheaded by the Beatles, whose early
style grafted onto a skiffle base the instrumental and vocal textures,
melodic structures, syncopated rhythms, and responsorial vocal styles of
early rock and roll, the modality and verse-refrain form of Anglo-Celtic
folk song, and some ornamental chromaticisms and triadic parallelisms
from late-nineteenth-century European harmony. Other leading expo-
nents included Gerry and the Pacemakers and the Searchers.[12]

As Moore points out, other Liverpool artists achieved international success in the 1960s, but the Beatles were the most successful practitioners
of this style.

AND THERE WAS MUSIC ...

During the early 1960s, the Beatles went through a series of personnel
changes before arriving at the final lineup: John Lennon (1940–1980),
rhythm guitar, lead guitar, bass guitar, keyboards, harmonica, voice;

James Paul McCartney (b. 1942), bass guitar, lead guitar, keyboards, drums, voice; George Harrison (1944–2001), lead guitar, bass guitar, sitar, keyboards, voice; and Ringo Starr (Richard Starkey) (b. 1940), drums, percussion, voice.[13] Although each member contributed original compositions to the group's recorded output, the principal composers were John Lennon and Paul McCartney, who between 1962 and 1969 wrote a total of 142 individually composed songs and 17 distinct collaborations.[14]

The Beatles' works can be comfortably grouped into three distinct style periods that correspond to the group's remarkable compositional development between the years 1962 and 1969:

1. Early Period: 1962–1964 (*consolidation*)
2. Middle Period: 1965–1966 (*experimentation*)
3. Late Period: 1967–1969 (*extended forms*)

The early period (1962–1964) was characterized by a consolidation of musical elements inherited from previous eras. The Beatles then integrated these elements into a highly distinctive personal style which featured: (1) novel approaches to vocal harmony that tended to include intervals of 4ths and 5ths as opposed to the more conventional 3rds and 6ths (*Baby's in Black*—1964); (2) the blending of rock and blues inflections with elements derived from country-western or folk styles (*You Can't Do That*—1964; *She's a Woman*—1964); (3) an enduring fascination with the popular ballad style (*Till There Was You*—1963; *And I Love Her*—1964; *If I Fell*—1964); and (4) the incorporation of innovative vocal and instrumental sound gestures into the structure of their songs (*Love Me Do*—1962; *She Loves You*—1963; *I Feel Fine*—1964). The early period is thus largely distinguished by a gradual mastery of established popular musical forms.[15]

The middle period (1965–1966) is characterized by a noticeable increase in stylistic experimentation. On their early records, the band members had relied heavily on producer George Martin to provide instrumental flourishes that lay beyond the scope of their own technical abilities. At this point however, they began to regularly employ studio musicians in an effort to realize their increasingly complex musical ideas. The first instance of this development occurs on the 1965 album

Help! where session musician Johnnie Scott plays the distinctive alto and tenor flute lines that grace the coda of John Lennon's "You've Got to Hide Your Love Away."[16] On the same album, "Yesterday" features a string quartet, which provides a tasteful and effective backdrop to Paul McCartney's solo guitar and vocal performance.[17]

This trend continues on *Revolver* (1966), which features a brass section on "Got to Get You Into My Life," a string octet on "Eleanor Rigby," and a French horn solo by Alan Civil on "For No One."[18] In addition to an expanded approach to instrumentation, the sessions for *Revolver* were also characterized by an increased interest in the musical possibilities engendered by multitrack recording technology. This is evident in several innovative tracks from the *Revolver* sessions:

1. "I'm Only Sleeping"—Guitar parts recorded backwards are featured throughout the track.[19]
2. "Rain"—Tape-reversed vocal tracks are looped in to become prominent during the song's coda.[20]
3. "Tomorrow Never Knows"—A series of exotic tape loops form the backdrop of the song proper and are "played" through the studio console during the final mix.[21]

The idiosyncratic nature of these recordings along with the groundbreaking sessions for "Penny Lane" and "Strawberry Fields Forever" in late 1966 helped pave the way for the formal and technical experimentation that would characterize the late period (1967–1969).

As we've seen, the Beatles' early career was characterized by a gradual mastery of the popular musical forms inherited from previous eras. By 1966, however, one can sense the group's increasing frustration with the limitations of the popular song. If *Rubber Soul* represents a near-perfect balance of form and content, then *Revolver* is the moment at which the content of the Beatles' work begins to overwhelm the limitations of their inherited forms. Subsequent releases attempt to resolve this dilemma in a variety of interesting and innovative ways.

The band employs an overarching concept on *Sgt. Pepper's Lonely Hearts Club Band* in an apparent effort to unify individual tracks. As a result, the average length of each song increases while thematic lyrical development becomes integrated into the group's compositional style.

Magical Mystery Tour attempts to elaborate on the *Sgt. Pepper* sound by focusing almost exclusively on the idea of texture as an important compositional element. On *The Beatles* (LP), the fundamental theme is incongruity, as the principle of organic unity is increasingly called into question.[22] *Get Back* seems closely related to its predecessor in its tendency to foreground musical process.[23] Finally, there is *Abbey Road*, the Beatles' final recorded work, and with it comes the proposed solution to the formal dilemma first encountered three years earlier.

ABBEY ROAD

In the two years prior to the release of *Abbey Road*, the Beatles, though still growing creatively, were going through a slow process of internal disintegration. The acrimony and infighting that characterized the sessions for *The Beatles* (LP) had increased steadily during the recording and filming of *Get Back*, causing many to wonder if the group would soon disband. In the book, *At the Apple's Core: The Beatles from the Inside*, film producer Denis O'Dell (*A Hard Day's Night, Magical Mystery Tour, Let It Be*) described the group's difficulties at this time:

> Communication—or the lack of it—was at the heart of the problem. Throughout my career as a producer I had seen many major creative disagreements: arguments between leading stars and actors, between stars and directors, directors and designers, designers and camera crews. I've even been involved in a few myself. Such clashes are usually resolved, often very quickly, to the mutual satisfaction of all concerned and mostly to the benefit of the film. In short, disagreements are frequently productive. But this wasn't the case with the Beatles. They would never thrash out their differences with each other (or anyone else for that matter) in any sort of constructive or reasonable way. Instead, they would simply stop communicating with one another. Nothing ever got resolved, and the awkward silences formed a breeding ground for hostility and resentment.[24]

In the months following the conclusion of *Get Back*, a series of low-intensity recording sessions took place as individual group members carefully pondered their next move. Finally, McCartney decided to contact producer George Martin concerning the possibility of working together again on another album. Martin described his reaction to this request:

Let It Be [*Get Back*] was such an unhappy record (even though there are some great songs on it) that I really believed that was the end of the Beatles, and I assumed that I would never work with them again. I thought, "What a shame to end like this." So I was quite surprised when Paul rang me up and said, "We're going to make another record—would you like to produce it?" My immediate answer was "Only if you let me produce it the way we used to." He said, "We will, we want to,"—"John included?"—"Yes, honestly." So I said, "Well, if you really want to, let's do it. Let's get together again." It was a very happy record. I guess it was happy because everybody thought it was going to be the last.[25]

By all accounts, the sessions for *Abbey Road* were relatively magnanimous. Individual egos were subsumed for the sake of the music, and, for the first time since the glory days of 1966–1967, all four of the band members are featured on nearly every track. Following an impressive set of polished and stylistically varied material, the album concludes with an extended series of song fragments that constitute the bulk of the album's second side.

George Harrison described the renewed sense of unity regarding the recording of the *Abbey Road* medley: "During the album things got a bit more positive, and although it had some overdubs, we got to play the whole medley. We put them in order, played the backing track and recorded it all in one take, going from one arrangement to the next. We did actually perform more like musicians again."[26] Ringo Starr shared Harrison's sentiments and had this to say: "After the *Let It Be* nightmare, *Abbey Road* turned out fine. The second side is brilliant. Out of the ashes of all that madness, that last section for me is one of the finest pieces we put together.[27]

But some conflicts did emerge, the most memorable being a disagreement concerning the album's final running order. Lennon, it seems, was resistant to McCartney and Martin's ideas for the medley. Allegedly, he wanted all of his songs on one side of the record and all of McCartney's on the other.[28] Nevertheless, the results of the sessions for what would be the group's final recorded work were evidently satisfying for all those concerned. In *The Beatles' Anthology*, Martin recounts:

I tried with Paul to get back into the old *Pepper* way of creating something really worthwhile, and we put together the long side. John objected very much to what we did on the second side of *Abbey Road*, which was almost entirely Paul and [me] working together, with contribution from the others. John always was a Teddy Boy. He was a rock 'n' roller and wanted a number of individual tracks. So we compromised. But even on the second side, John helped. He would come and put his little bit in and have an idea for sewing a bit of music into the tapestry. Everyone worked frightfully well, and that's why I'm very fond of it.[29]

POSTSCRIPT

So, was the *Abbey Road* medley truly the artistic triumph that the Beatles and their collaborators considered it to be? In subsequent chapters, we will attempt to answer this question by means of an eclectic method of analysis designed to generate useful data with regard to the various elements of sound, form, and reference.

NOTES

It should be noted that the material in this chapter is not intended as a definitive biography; rather, it is designed to facilitate discussions of form and reference that are essential elements of subsequent chapters. The reader should refer to various extant biographical materials on the Beatles listed in the bibliography.

1. A series of original musical and spoken-word recordings released at Christmas to the Beatles' official fan club from 1963 through 1969. Mark Lewisohn, *The Beatles Recording Sessions* (New York: Harmony Books, 1988), 88.

2. Hunter Davies, *The Beatles* (New York: W.W. Norton, 1978), 208.

3. *The Beatles Anthology*, DVD, directed by Geoff Wonfor (London: Apple Corps Limited, 2003).

4. Beatles, *Anthology* (San Francisco: Chronicle Books, 2000), 229

5. "Meeting the Press," *A Hard Day's Night*, DVD, directed by Richard Lester (1964; Burbank, CA: Miramax Home Entertainment, 2002), dialogue transcribed by author.

6. Mark Lewisohn, *The Beatles' Recording Sessions* (New York: Harmony Books, 1988), 88.

7. The Beatles, *The Beatles' Christmas Album* (Apple LYN 2154, 1970), dialogue transcribed by author.

8. Ed Sikov, *Mr. Strangelove: A Biography of Peter Sellers* (New York: Hyperion, 2002), 59.

9. Peter Brown, in discussion with the author, Aug. 5, 2003.

10. Brown, in discussion with the author, Aug. 5, 2003.

11. Paul McCartney, in particular, was very adept at this process and often learned the more obscure B-sides of various records in order to give the early Beatles a more specialized, less typical set list. Lewisohn, *Recording Sessions*, 8.

12. Stanley Sadie, ed., *The New Grove Dictionary of Music and Musicians, Second Edition, Volume Three* (New York: Thames & Hudson, 2001), 24–25.

13. Sadie, ed., *New Grove Dictionary, Volume Three*, 21.

14. Per Myrsten, "Who Is the Main Composer of the Beatles' Songs?" *Soundscapes.Info*, vol. 2, Oct. 1999, http://www.icce.rug.nl/~soundscapes/VOLUME02/Beatlesongs.html (July 15, 2007).

15. Terence J. O'Grady, *The Beatles: A Musical Evolution* (Boston: Twayne Publishers, 1983), 64–65.

16. Lewisohn, *Recording Sessions*, 55.

17. Lewisohn, *Recording Sessions*, 59.

18. Lewisohn, *Recording Sessions*, 77–79.

19. Lewisohn, *Recording Sessions*, 78.

20. Lewisohn, *Recording Sessions*, 74.

21. Lewisohn, *Recording Sessions*, 72.

22. Known by popular consensus as *The White Album*, *The Beatles* (1968) is arguably a more fully realized conceptual statement than *Sgt. Pepper's Lonely Hearts Club Band* since its central theme grows organically from within the work, whereas the *Pepper* concept is imposed on individual songs from without.

23. Eventually released as the album *Let It Be* (1970).

24. Denis O'Dell, *At the Apple's Core: The Beatles from the Inside* (London: Peter Owen Ltd., 2002), 140–41.

25. Beatles, *Anthology*, 337.

26. Beatles, *Anthology*, 338.

27. Beatles, Anthology, 337.

28. Lewisohn, *Recording Sessions*, 193.

29. Beatles, *Anthology*, 338.

3

METHODS AND TECHNIQUES OF ANALYSIS

The method of analysis to be implemented on the *Abbey Road* medley is an adaptation of the eclectic method formulated by Lawrence Ferrara in *Philosophy and the Analysis of Music*. This approach incorporates concepts rooted in the philosophies of Edmund Husserl, Martin Heidegger, and Susanne K. Langer and provides a methodology that enables the analyst to more fully engage an artwork at various levels of significance. Specifically, the goal is to develop a means of analysis that allows one to position the various aspects of referential meaning within the more discernible levels of musical syntax and time.

Ferrara's approach is predicated upon the notion that researchers tend to establish their methods first and then proceed to the examination of a musical work. While such a strategy allows for a certain amount of presumed objectivity, it also tends to mitigate the full significance of the work under study. The researcher thus becomes preoccupied with the execution of the chosen method at the expense of the work itself.

In response to this problem, Ferrara's eclectic method allows various analytical levels to function independently while at the same time contributing to an integrated understanding of a musical work. In keeping with this approach, the analysis of the *Abbey Road* medley in part II of this book is designed to clarify the relationships that connect the various elements of sound, form, and reference.

In this chapter, elements listed under the heading Musical Syntax focus on the analysis of musical structure in both the traditional and popular style. Those listed under Sound-in-Time deal with phenomenological approaches to musical analysis. Elements listed under the heading, Referential Meaning focus on models for the analysis of the literary work, theories of the symbolic or representational qualities of music, and philosophical approaches regarding the "onto-historical world of the composer."[1]

MUSICAL SYNTAX

Since one of the goals of this book is to explore the continuity of the *Abbey Road* medley with previous compositional styles, I refer to various texts that deal with the analysis of formal development in Western Music. In this regard, Nicholas Cook's *A Guide to Musical Analysis* was of particular importance. Cook's work not only provides a scholarly overview of various analytical strategies, it is also notable for its refusal to shy away from the weaknesses inherent in each of those strategies. One of the approaches that Cook discusses in depth is the Linear Reductive Analysis of Heinrich Schenker.[2]

Simply stated, Schenkerian analysis attempts to explain the organic qualities of "common-practice" tonal music. For Schenker, this organic quality is primarily achieved through a directed tonal motion in which the relationship between tonic and dominant harmony is the elemental principle, that is, the fundamental structure. Schenker's linear reductive method stresses the hierarchical relationships that exist among various musical elements. His method also attempts to describe the concinnity that results when these elements reappear at different levels of the musical structure.[3]

Although problematic when applied to post-tonal works, Schenker's ideas have proven very useful in the analysis of popular music. In recent studies, theorists such as Allan F. Moore and Walter Everett have applied post-Schenkerian principles to works by the Beatles.[4] In particular, Everett's two-volume set *The Beatles as Musicians* successfully employs linear reductive methods as part of a detailed study of the Beatles' entire recorded output.[5] Within the context of an eclectic analysis of the *Abbey Road* medley, post-Schenkerian methods can be seen as a valuable tool for establishing an acceptable standard of analytical objectivity.

THE SOUND-IN-TIME

Phenomenology attempts to orient itself toward the elemental qualities of human experience. To experience a phenomenon in this way requires the bracketing out of all that is not essential to it.[6] The philosopher Edmund Husserl pursued the development of phenomenology as a pure investigation into the nature and content of human consciousness. The tenets of his approach stress the bracketing of natural beliefs in order to more fully understand their structural sources. Building on elements found in the work of Immanuel Kant, Georg Wilhelm Friedrich Hegel, and Franz Brentano, Husserl sought to provide the field of phenomenology with a workable method of analysis.[7] Toward this end, he developed two phenomenological reductions:

1. Epoche—A suspension of the natural attitude. Here, the analyst attempts to bracket out all previous assumptions or prejudices connected to the work.
2. Eidetic—An attempt by the analyst to engage the essential characteristics of the work. This type of engagement will never be referential or formal in nature.[8]

Through the use of these reductions, the analyst may gain a unique insight into the growth and development that exists in a musical work.

REFERENTIAL MEANING

The analysis of referential meaning in the arts still provokes considerable controversy. Formal theorists often contend that attempts at assessing referential meaning do not lead to analytical clarity; rather, they produce a loss of empirical confirmation and, furthermore, a concomitant loss of control. They also assert that such methods are highly questionable since they may produce widely varying and, thus, unreliable results. Referentialists dispute this point by claiming that the same can be said of formal methods of analysis. Referentialists note that artworks are undeniably expressive of human feeling as well as the cultural world of the artist.[9] In an effort to circumvent this impasse, a series of twentieth-century philosophers have looked for ways to systematically assess referential meaning in the arts.

Roman Ingarden studied philosophy with Edmund Husserl. Although his training was mainly phenomenological, Ingarden ultimately directed his work toward ontology.[10] His best-known and most influential text is *The Literary Work of Art*, first published in 1931. Here, Ingarden asserts that every literary work is constituted of four distinct layers: (1) word sounds and phonetic formations; (2) meaning units—from the individual meanings of words to the higher-order of phrases, sentences, paragraphs, and so on; (3) represented objectivities—the visual or auditory aspects, which constitute the world that the reader actively constructs in consciousness; and (4) schematized aspects—the visual or auditory aspects not specifically represented in the work that nevertheless may be apprehended by the reader.[11] Each of these four layers leaves room for its own particular kind of aesthetic value, and thus provides a framework within which the analyst can create detailed discussions of literary works by foregrounding their various levels of textual significance.[12] Ingarden's approach will be adapted for use in the section of the analysis of the *Abbey Road* medley that focuses on musical and textual representation.

Susanne K. Langer's work proposed a new paradigm for the analysis of poetic meaning in the arts.[13] Responding to the view that the arts were not worthy of serious scholarship, she asserted that art forms such as music should properly be regarded as nondiscursive symbol systems that capture the general forms and concepts of human life and feeling.[14] For Langer, musical meaning cannot be fully understood based on the rules of ordinary language.[15] In the book *Philosophy In a New Key*, she writes: "Because the forms of human feeling are much more congruent with musical forms than with the forms of language, music can *reveal* the nature of feelings with a detail and truth that language cannot approach."[16]

Although Langer's work in 1942 is somewhat problematic due to her roots in modernist notions of "music" as Western European classical music, she does create a viable starting point for the further exploration of meaning in the arts. Her work provides the basis for the section of the eclectic analysis of the *Abbey Road* medley that focuses on discussions of virtual feeling.[17]

Martin Heidegger claimed that referential meaning in art is only possible when the analyst remains "open" and responsive to the work in question.[18] Building on the philosophy of Edmund Husserl, Heidegger described how listeners understand the "life-world" of a composer of the past through the historical traditions that embody both.[19] The sections of this book that deal with the onto-historical world of the Beatles stress the necessity of placing the *Abbey Road* medley within the group's own cultural context in order to clarify their enduring relevance for the contemporary listener. Heidegger's ideas are also pertinent to the shift in musical praxis that followed the incorporation of recording techniques into the compositional process. The resulting reification of the "musical canvas" (described in chapter 1 of this book) has intriguing implications with regard to Heidegger's model of the dynamic interaction that exists between work materials and referential meaning in a work of art.[20]

THE ECLECTIC METHOD

The nine steps of my adaptation of Ferrara's eclectic method are listed below and then discussed individually in greater detail. It should be noted that in addition to providing a qualitative analysis of a complete transcription of the *Abbey Road* medley, this adaptation also includes a discussion of recording techniques used in the creation of the work. Considering the ways in which the Beatles engaged the recording medium as a part of their compositional process, I deemed this incorporation essential in order to fully assess the significance of the *Abbey Road* medley.

Historical Background

This step presents biographical information about the artist and/or the work in question. This aspect of the analysis will attempt to place the *Abbey Road* medley within an appropriate historical framework. Since much of this material has already been discussed in the overview of the Beatles' musical career presented in chapter 2, this step will offer insights into the placement of the work within the development of the Beatles' creative dynamic.

Open Listenings

The second step consists of a series of listening events guided by Edmund Husserl's principle of *epoche*—that is, the suspension of the natural attitude in an effort to provide a clarification of one's pre-understanding.[21] Here, the analyst attempts to bracket out all preexisting judgments (positive or negative) related to the work in question. At this level, the analyst is encouraged to avoid censoring thoughts or feelings in order to provide as unbiased a discussion as possible.

Musical Syntax/Recording Strategies

In the third step, a conventional method of analysis is applied to the work. The syntactical analysis of the *Abbey Road* medley will employ harmonic, motivic, and post-Schenkerian methods within the framework of a systematic approach to the work as outlined by Nicholas Cook in *A Guide to Musical Analysis*. The main body of the analysis will employ a section-by-section breakdown modeled on the work of Donald Francis Tovey.[22] As previously noted, I have adapted this step to include a detailed discussion of recording technique in order to ascertain its possible impact on the compositional process.[23]

The Sound-in-Time

During this important step, the analyst attempts to engage the work from a purely descriptive phenomenological perspective.[24] The purpose of this type of analysis is "to heighten our awareness for the perception of the experience."[25] As a result, things normally dismissed as subjective would be described for their own sake.

Musical and Textual Representation

At the fifth level of my adaptation of the eclectic method of analysis, I will report on various referential meanings that exist within the program or text of the work. This level consists of an adaptation of the methodology described by Roman Ingarden in *The Literary Work of Art*. My adaptation of Ingarden's theories will subsume the four strata previously described into a two-pronged approach intended to assess the text in terms of *surface structure* (syntax) and *deep structure* (semantics). As in the other aspects of the referential analysis (virtual feeling, onto-historical worlds), the goal here is to ground the data generated within the levels of musical syntax and the sound-in-time.

Virtual Feeling

Using the work of Susanne K. Langer as a guide, the sixth step will attempt to engage the work in terms of its qualities as a symbolic system, the function of which is to create virtual forms for human feeling. At this level of the analysis, one is encouraged to employ poetic or metaphorical descriptions in an effort to properly describe the virtual feeling or feelings conveyed by the work.

Onto-historical Worlds

During the seventh step, the analyst attempts to describe how the work expresses the onto-historical world of the composer, that is, the world of a cultural people. In *Philosophy and the Analysis of Music*, Ferrara describes this process.

> One's present is in a stream of history that connects the past and the future. The historical life-world that surrounds a composer of the past is connected to contemporary listeners and their present through the historical tradition that encompasses both. The contemporary person listens to music through the stylistic and expressive norms that have developed in the historical tradition in which his past and present are conjoined.[26]

As a result, the time and place in which an analysis occurs affect what a musical work *can mean*. At this level, the analyst is once again encouraged to employ poetry and metaphor in order to properly describe the ontology conveyed by the work.

Open Listenings

The eighth step is characterized by a return to the process of open listening first described in step 2. Once again, the analyst is guided by Edmund Husserl's principle of *epoche*—that is, the suspension of the natural attitude—in an effort to provide a clarification of pre-understanding.[27] At this point however, the various levels of musical significance discussed in the preceding steps are allowed to flow together in what Ferrara describes as "a dynamic and polyphonic tapestry."[28]

Meta-critique

In an effort to improve the quality of subsequent research, the ninth step provides a critique of the inherent strengths and weaknesses of the chosen method and its impact upon the analysis of the musical work. This step can include recommendations for future research.[29] In this book, however, such recommendations are presented in chapter 9, immediately following a detailed discussion of the data generated by an eclectic analysis of the *Abbey Road* medley.

NOTES

1. Lawrence Ferrara, *Philosophy and the Analysis of Music* (New York: Greenwood Press, 1991), 184.
2. Nicholas Cook, *A Guide to Musical Analysis* (New York: G. Braziller, 1987), 27–66.
3. Allen Clayton Cadwallader and David Gagné, *Analysis of Tonal Music: A Schenkerian Approach* (New York: Oxford University Press, 1998), v–viii.
4. Allan F. Moore, *The Beatles:* Sgt. Pepper's Lonely Hearts Club Band (New York: Cambridge University Press, 1997).
5. Walter Everett, *The Beatles as Musicians: The Quarry Men Through* Rubber Soul (New York: Oxford University Press, 2001); Walter Everett, *The Beatles as Musicians:* Revolver *Through* The Anthology (New York: Oxford University Press, 1999).
6. Cook, *A Guide to Musical Analysis*, 67.
7. Ferrara, *Philosophy and the Analysis of Music*, 63.
8. Ferrara, *Philosophy and the Analysis of Music*, 64–66.
9. Ferrara, *Philosophy and the Analysis of Music*, xiii–xxi.

10. Ferrara, *Philosophy and the Analysis of Music*, 168.

11. Ferrara, *Philosophy and the Analysis of Music*, 168–70.

12. Amie Thomasson, "Roman Ingarden," *The Stanford Encyclopedia of Philosophy* (Spring 2004 Edition), http://plato.stanford.edu/archives/spr2004/entries/ingarden/ (July 15, 2007).

13. Ferrara, *Philosophy and the Analysis of Music*, 16.

14. Susanne K. Langer, *Feeling and Form: A Theory of Art* (New York: Scribner, 1953), 27.

15. Ferrara, *Philosophy and the Analysis of Music*, 14–15.

16. Susanne K. Langer, *Philosophy in a New Key: Aa Study in the Symbolism of Reason, Rite and Art* (Cambridge, MA: Harvard University Press, 1951), 235.

17. Further explorations of meaning in music can be found in the following works: Deryck Cooke, *The Language of Music* (New York: Oxford University Press, 1959); Wilson Coker, *Music and Meaning: A Theoretical Introduction to Musical Aesthetics* (New York: The Free Press, 1972); Peter Kivy, *The Corded Shell: Reflections on Musical Expression* (Princeton, NJ: Princeton University Press, 1980).

18. Ferrara, *Philosophy and the Analysis of Music*, 123–41.

19. Ferrara, *Philosophy and the Analysis of Music*, 16.

20. Ferrara, *Philosophy and the Analysis of Music*, 135–38.

21. Ferrara, *Philosophy and the Analysis of Music*, 64.

22. Sir Donald Francis Tovey, *A Companion to Beethoven's Pianoforte Sonatas* (London: The Associated Board of the R. A. M. and R. C. M., 1931).

23. I have elected to place this discussion at the end of the syntactical analysis to facilitate a smooth transition from the discussion of musical syntax to an analysis of the sound-in-time.

24. Ferrara, *Philosophy and the Analysis of Music*, 182–83.

25. Ferrara, *Philosophy and the Analysis of Music*, 67.

26. Ferrara, *Philosophy and the Analysis of Music*, xvi–xvii.

27. Ferrara, *Philosophy and the Analysis of Music*, 64.

28. Ferrara, *Philosophy and the Analysis of Music*, 184–85.

29. Ferrara, Philosophy and the Analysis of Music, 186.

Part II

AN ECLECTIC ANALYSIS
OF THE *ABBEY ROAD* MEDLEY

4

PRELUDE—"BECAUSE"

STEP ONE—HISTORICAL BACKGROUND

The basic track of "Because" was recorded at Abbey Road Studio Two on August 1, 1969. Subsequent recording, overdubbing, and mixing sessions took place at Studios Two and Three at the Abbey Road Studios on August 4, 5,[1] and 12, 1969.[2]

"Because" has often been described as a parody of Beethoven's Moonlight Sonata, Op. 27, No. 2, and an examination of the similarities between the two works tends to support this claim.[3] In particular, the arpeggiated C# minor triads, and the subsequent shift to the flat supertonic (Neapolitan), suggest the influence of Beethoven. Largely the creation of John Lennon with possible input from producer George Martin,[4] the work's true significance may lie in the fact that it is the last example in the Beatles' musical corpus of an intriguing creative dynamic that had developed between John Lennon and Paul McCartney.

As the Beatles' principal songwriter from 1962 to 1965, Lennon set the pace for various developments in the group's approach to musical structure and lyrical content. As the emerging half of a fruitful songwriting partnership, Paul McCartney tended to provide stylistic relief to the rhythm and blues focus of Lennon's early contributions. By 1966, however, McCartney began to dominate the group's subsequent creative direction, and it was at this point that Lennon also began to find a new role.

Despite his acknowledged musical brilliance, McCartney had a tendency to linger too long at various creative levels. Once a breakthrough was attained, he seemed more content to produce works in a similar vein rather than push the creative envelope. This contrasted sharply with Lennon, who had a fundamentally impatient nature and tended to look for creative departures as a matter of course. In the wake of McCartney's mid-period ascendancy, Lennon began to produce works that essentially challenged his partner's complacency and urged him to move to ever-higher creative levels.

On *Revolver* (1966), Lennon seems to be struggling to extract some new expressive effects from the forms he'd been working with since 1965. As McCartney continued to explore a variety of styles and genres in tracks like "Eleanor Rigby" and "Got to Get You into My Life," Lennon presents material here that is even less inspired than the contributions of George Harrison—who at this point is just beginning to emerge as a viable songwriter. The most notable exception to this alarming trend is "Tomorrow Never Knows," in which Lennon departs from his inherited rhythm-and-blues style to pursue full-blown avant-garde experimentation. The resulting track is colored with a collection of tape loops assembled by McCartney and fed directly into the recording console. The various loops were then played during the final mix to form a timbral backwash to the song proper.[5] This innovative approach to multitrack recording clearly points toward the conceptual development evident on the group's next album, *Sgt. Pepper's Lonely Hearts Club Band* (1967).

Sgt. Pepper isn't quite the album that it claims to be. Despite the reappearance of the title track near the end of side two, there is little evidence of thematic or harmonic relationship between any of the tracks. Here, rather than attempting to create a bona fide concept album, the Beatles seem to be saying, "Look everyone! Concept albums are possible. This album isn't it, but it proves that it's possible!" As on *Revolver*, McCartney once again dominates with a collection of genre studies, which are still remarkable for their tuneful ingenuity. But the most significant track is Lennon's "A Day in the Life." Essentially a classically conceived structure with sections of breathtaking aleatoric improvisation by full orchestra, this track paves the way for the group's next big creative leap, *The Beatles* (LP) (1968).

Although *Sgt. Pepper* tends to get most of the mainstream praise, it is *The Beatles* (LP) that continues to inspire younger generations of musicians with its sprawling song sequence, its carefree approach to genre and style, and its blatant disregard for popular musical conventions.[6] Here, Lennon presents two new works that would greatly influence subsequent developments in the group's recorded output. The first, "Happiness Is a Warm Gun," is the blueprint for much of what takes place in the *Abbey Road* medley, in that it seems to have been the model employed by McCartney for the composition of Movement I ("You Never Give Me Your Money"). It is also the first example of a through-composed work in the Beatles' entire catalog, as four contrasting sections are presented in just over two minutes. Building directly on the progressive elements of "A Day in the Life" and "Tomorrow Never Knows," Lennon also presents a viable sound collage with "Revolution 9." Seemingly inspired by Karlheinz Stockhausen's *Hymnen* (1967), Lennon's work is remarkable for its insight into the narrative functions of recorded sound.[7] At just under nine minutes in length, "Revolution 9" is the longest track the group had released to this point and thus begins to create the formal space necessary to prepare the listener for the multipart structure of the *Abbey Road* medley.

As the final track recorded for the *Abbey Road* album, "Because" functions on various levels of significance. Its curious tone of what might be described as secular religiosity probably gave the *Abbey Road* sessions an appropriate sense of closure. The sparse instrumentation is certainly a welcome relief after the complex textures that characterize much of the album. However, in contrast with its surface elements, the song also employs an ingenious musical structure that not only creates an appropriate setting for the poetry of the text but also portends some of the more complex harmonic relationships employed in the main sections of the medley. Here, Lennon raises the bar for the last time, setting the standard for future Beatles albums that were never to come.

STEP TWO—OPEN LISTENINGS

The work is performed in a slow tempo. The introduction is played on what seems to be a harpsichord reiterating a slow, circular pattern that perhaps suggests the path to a transcendent mental state. The entrance of the vocal harmony two measures before the beginning of the A section is a breathtaking moment that contributes to the general feeling of timelessness. From here until the end of the piece, the regularity of the eighth-note pattern in the accompaniment contrasts sharply with the ethereal mystery evoked by the vocal melody and text. This duality does much to foster a sense of hymnlike awe and wonder.

The B section is marked by a move to the interpersonal and thereby creates a sense of the here and now. This effect is short-lived, however, as the A section soon returns with new lyrical material that reemphasizes the circularity at work within the piece. This section then develops into a vocal/instrumental dialogue that attempts to resolve the philosophical questions posed by the narrative. This dialogue is not literal, but tonal, as the melismatic vocal lines respond to the persistence of the instrumental phrasing. By ending on an unresolved harmony, the composer suggests that these fundamental questions are unanswerable and, therefore, an eternal source of wonder.

STEP THREE—MUSICAL SYNTAX

Key: C# minor
Meter: 4/4
Form: Strophic–Binary ‖: A (verses) :‖ B (refrain) :‖
Intro (verse) | Verse |
| Verse | Bridge |
| Verse | Verse / Coda

The musical form of "Because" is a combination of *strophic* and *binary*, which is often referred to as the *refrain form*. The verse melody appears twice as A, and A' before the appearance of B (refrain). Following the refrain, the A section returns, initially as a setting for verse 3, and then as part of an intriguing wordless coda in which fragments of the verse melody (in instrumental form) alternate with a melismatic three-part vocal line that varies and develops motivic material from section A.

The harmonic bed of the A section [i—ii°—V—VI—i—VI (V / bII)—bII–V(?)] is also used for the introduction at mm. 1–8. This introduction is eight measures long and breaks down into 2 sub-phrases of equal length. The Baldwin spinet electric harpsichord opens on an arpeggiation of the tonic minor (C#) in 3+3+2 grouping that slowly winds its way toward the dominant (G#) by way of a diminished triad on scale degree 2. The composer then presents a deceptive cadence on VI (m. 5), as the arpeggiated pattern subtly adapts itself to the new harmony.

On beat 4 of measure 5, an electric guitar enters doubling the keyboard. In addition to emphasizing the original line and thus thickening the texture, the entrance of the guitar serves to enhance the expressiveness of the music by expanding its spatiotemporal dimensions. This is followed by a 4-measure transition that briefly tonicizes the flat supertonic and sets up the arrival of verse I.

Example 1.   Prelude "Because"—Intro (4-measure transition)[8]

The verse itself is arranged in phrase groups of 4+4+2 measures and precisely follows the harmonic structure of the Introduction as the foundation for a three-part melodic line, which begins at measure 10.

Example 2.   Prelude "Because"—Phrase I of Verse

The thematic material consists of a disjunctive melodic pattern that outlines the tonic triad. This material follows the harmonic progression and is echoed in the keyboard accompaniment pattern in diminution.

Example 3.   Prelude "Because"—Accompaniment Pattern and Melodic Line

During the recording session each part of the vocal harmony was sung three times, thus creating a nine-voice choir on the finished recording. As well as thickening the overall musical texture, this effect also contributes to a general obfuscation of the melodic line.

The end of the Introduction (A) creates a fascinating ambiguity as to how one should properly identify the function of the chord in measure 10 (D–F–G#).

As Walter Everett points out in *The Beatles as Musicians: Revolver through the Anthology*, one would normally expect a full dominant chord (V) following a lowered II in order to create the appropriate cadence in C# minor. The chord at measure 10, however, confounds conventional expectations and only reveals its true function at the end of the second verse where it appears as an applied vii° of a structural IV (F#).[9]

The thematic material of the refrain (B) consists of a conjunct melodic pattern that serves to diffuse the tension established in the verse sections.

The new B section (refrain) is four measures long and completes the overall motion toward a structural V (mm. 33–34). A change in texture is also noted with the entrance of a Moog synthesizer that doubles the arpeggiated line of the harpsichord and electric guitar. As previously noted, the melody is now predominantly conjunct in keeping with the intimacy alluded to in the text. The vii° in measure 30 suggests the tonicization of F# and the music briefly conveys an appropriate sense of stability. This effect is short-lived however, as the move toward V (G#7) sets up the return of the tonic (C#) at measure 35.

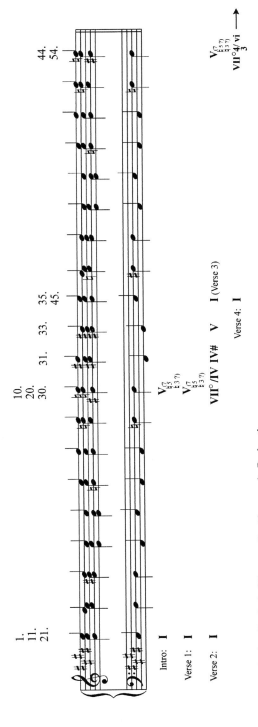

Example 4.   Prelude "Because"—Harmonic Reduction

Example 5.   Prelude "Because"—Thematic Material (Refrain)

Verse III restates the motivic material from earlier verses with little variation. At measure 41, however, the uppermost vocal harmony adds a remarkable ornamentation that employs a lower neighbor grace note.

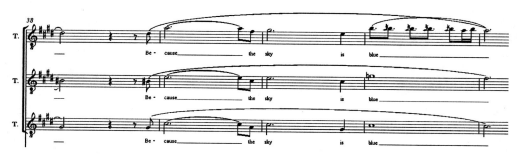

Example 6.   Prelude "Because"—Melodic Material (Verse III)

At measure 43, all three vocal parts then vary the motivic material that originally appeared in mm. 9–10, mm. 19–20, and mm. 29–30:

Example 7.   Prelude "Because"—Motivic Variation (mm. 43–45)

The variation heard at the end of verse III continues in verse IV (coda) as the three-part vocal line engages in an intricate duet with the Moog synthesizer, which restates the motivic material from the verses:

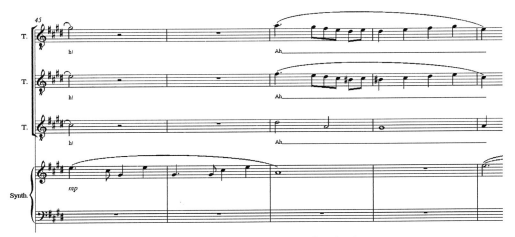

Example 8.   Prelude "Because"—Vocal Duet with Moog Synthesizer

The original phrase groups of 4+4+2 measures are now expanded within the context of the musical dialogue with the Moog synthesizer. They now appear as groups of 4+4+4+4+4 measures.[10] The duet continues throughout the verse-coda until the work concludes on measure 54. The concluding chord (vii°) that was previously featured in measures 10, 20, 30, and 44 now appears with a new function—as an applied vii° of A minor:

Example 9.   Prelude "Because"—Final Appearance of Diminished Seventh

The varying function of vii° is this work's most significant structural feature in that it provides, in its final appearance, a clear harmonic link with Movement I ("You Never Give Me Your Money"). It thereby lends credence to the argument that the *Abbey Road* medley exhibits structural relationships, which justify it being classified as a genuine example of extended form.

RECORDING STRATEGIES

During the sessions for the *White Album* (1968), the studio finally granted the Beatles full access to an 8-track recording console. Up to that point, the group's recordings were predominantly on 4-track.[11] Curiously, EMI had acquired a 3M model 8-track machine in early 1968 but was waiting for Francis Thompson (one of the chief technicians) to run a series of tests before installing it in the main studios. Upon learning that an 8-track unit was in the building, the Beatles promptly broke into Thompson's office and brought it down to Studio Two where it was used to record overdubs onto the existing 4-track takes of "While My Guitar Gently Weeps."[12]

The introduction of 8-track recording techniques meant that the musicians no longer had to limit their arrangements and production ideas in order to save space on the master tape. This resulted in fewer reduction mixes, and, consequently, the arrangements on *Abbey Road* are more varied than on any of the group's prior recordings. Additionally, an increase in textural depth is noted as extensive panning across the stereo spectrum is employed throughout to create a richly detailed aural picture.

In the case of "Because," the basic tracks of the Baldwin spinet electric harpsichord, electric guitar, and bass guitar were all recorded on August 1, 1969. During this session, Ringo Starr, who is otherwise not present on the finished recording, played a regular quarter-note pattern on the hi-hat cymbals in order to create a steady pulse for the players. Onto this basic track, the singers (Lennon, McCartney, and Harrison) added a lush three-part harmony vocal, which recalled earlier Beatles efforts such as "This Boy" (1963) and "Yes It Is" (1965). Producer George Martin guided the group through the intricate vocal arrangement and apparently suggested alterations and additions to the parts. The group then took full advantage of the newly acquired 8-track format by over-dubbing the three-part harmony twice more in order to create the effect of a nine-part choir.[13]

The nine-part vocal texture does much to contribute to the track's remarkable impact. The close microphone placement achieves a sense of intimacy that draws the listener powerfully into the complex texture. The melodic line itself is also remarkable for its dramatic use of caesuras at key structural moments, as well as its frequent use of melismatic ornamentation as an extension of the text, rather than facile substitution. It is also interesting to note that when "Because" was remixed for inclusion on *Anthology 3* (1995) to feature just the vocals without instrumental accompaniment, the track seemed to lose none of its considerable musical impact.

As with many of the tracks on *Abbey Road*, Prelude "Because" is also notable for its use of the Moog synthesizer.[14] During the final overdubbing sessions for the song on August 5, 1969, George Harrison used the Moog to double the keyboard/guitar ostinato in the B section and also created the distinctive waveform for the restatement of the main melodic line that is heard in the song's coda.[15]

The use of the Moog here is particularly noteworthy for its taste and restraint. Rather than exploiting the novelty of the instrument's exotic tonal effects, the band members chose instead to view it as a full-fledged member of the ensemble. As a result, they thicken the overall texture of the track in a way that seems natural and inevitable.

STEP FOUR—THE SOUND-IN-TIME

Out of the silence, an instrument that sounds like an amplified harpsichord enters on the left channel with a winding, maze-like motion. At 0:12, a guitar (electric) enters on the right playing the same circular pattern. This doubling is particularly noteworthy since the two instruments seem so well matched from the standpoint of pure sound. In addition, the guitar player seems to be at a distance. This effect, combined with the fact that the two instruments are playing the identical musical line, lends the music a three-dimensional quality similar to the perspective effects one finds in representational art.

At 0:24, male voices enter in a shimmering three-part vocal harmony that seems larger than life and proceeds to tower over the rest of the instrumentation. A deeply resonating bass guitar accompanies the voices. Between 0:28 and 0:30, voices and instruments assert a very unstable cluster that is decidedly unsettling on first listen. In the accompaniment, the aforementioned circular pattern ascends to its highest point, suddenly descends, and then stops.

At 0:30, the instruments restate the previous accompaniment pattern, while the vocal harmonies intone the text. The melody rises and falls in a manner that seems to echo the mazelike motion of the accompaniment. Between 1:01 and 1:24, the entire section is then repeated with new textual material. At 1:25, there is a move to a new contrasting section in which the various musical materials are less active. At this point, a distinctive instrumental timbre emerges suggesting the use of a French horn. But this is no ordinary horn. Its slightly distorted quality suggests that the instrument is visibly undulating with each note played.

At 1:42, the vocals and accompaniment return to present new textual material. For the most part, the sounds are consistent with the two statements heard earlier. At 2:00, however, the uppermost vocal part begins to shake in playful syncopation with the underlying rhythmic pulse. This remarkable brushstroke paves the way for an elegant duet between the three-part vocal harmony and the seeming French horn first heard in the previous section. The entire piece concludes at 2:44 with a restatement of the unstable tonal cluster heard earlier at 0:24, 0:54, and 1:24. The vocals and instrumental accompaniment then fade together into silence.

STEP FIVE—MUSICAL AND TEXTUAL REPRESENTATION

Because

Because the world is round it turns me on
Because the world is round . . . aaaahhh
Because the wind is high it blows my mind
Because the wind is high . . . aaaahhh
Love is all, love is new
Love is all, love is you.

> Because the sky is blue, it makes me cry
> Because the sky is blue . . . aaaahhh
> Aaaahhh. . . .

On the surface level, the text of Prelude "Because" exhibits a relatively straightforward use of long vowel sounds that are appropriate to the general mood of the musical setting. However, as one looks deeper, an intricate interplay of meaning is revealed in the underlying semantic structure. Of particular interest is the subtle duality created by the causal relationships expressed in each verse:

> Verse I: "the *world* is *round* it *turns* me on."
> Verse II: " the *wind* is *high* it *blows* my mind."
> Verse III: "the *sky* is *blue* it makes me *cry*."[16]

Here, the internal structure of the text illustrates the poet's awareness of the various qualities of Being that inform everyday language. Although the phrases in verses I and II were clichés, even when "Because" was first released, Lennon revitalizes them by focusing the listener's attention on the text's syntactical function. The work thereby creates a powerful metaphor for the human condition, which the listener then experiences on the surface of the text.

STEP SIX—VIRTUAL FEELING

The opening phrase, an arpeggiated pattern played on harpsichord, creates a dark sense of foreboding and effectively sets the mood for the struggle that is to follow. The tonal similarity to Beethoven's *Moonlight Sonata* has been duly noted. During the consequent phrase, an electric guitar doubles the harpsichord arpeggio. Placed back in the mix, the guitar line creates an effective sense of depth as the overall sonic picture gradually comes into focus. Lennon quickly makes adjustments to the Beethoven model and cadences at measure 9 in the key of the flat supertonic. At this point, a melismatic nine-part harmony creates a wondrous sense of relief that is short-lived, for in measure 10, the voices create a caesura over a diminished triad that precedes the entry of the first verse in the key of C# minor.

The first verse describes the singer's sense of wonder concerning the elemental properties of his life-world:

> Because the world is round it turns me on
> Because the world is round . . . aaaahhh

The musical setting repeats the opening arpeggio figure, while the melody casts an enchanting spell as it outlines the root position tonic triad. One senses the creation of sacred space, as the upper voice breaks free in measure 13 with a melisma that develops the motivic material first heard in measure 10.

The second verse continues with its description of the spirituality at the heart of natural wonder:

> Because the wind is high it blows my mind
> Because the wind is high . . . aaaahhh

In the first line (measures 20–24), Lennon effects a poetic transformation of the hackneyed counterculture phrase, "it blows my mind." By creating a causal relationship with "the wind," he manages to revitalize a well-worn cliché by restoring its syntactical function. The final melisma (measure 29) dovetails seamlessly into the B section. The arrival of B (measure 30) provides the spatiotemporal relief promised in measure 9.

> Love is all, love is new
> Love is all, love is you.

A synthesizer enters doubling the harpsichord/guitar figure and helps ground the work with a rich textural stability. Because of the harmonic rhythm, F# major feels at first like a true modulation, but very quickly we realize that it is actually the subdominant of our original key (C# minor) and that we are moving back toward the opening motive. The firm dominant function of the G# major chord in measure 33 provides the strongest cadence yet and makes the return of the circular motive less threatening. The listener can now wholeheartedly embrace the mystery of which the poet sings.

> Because the sky is blue, it makes me cry
> Because the sky is blue . . . aaaahhh
> Aaaahhh. . . .

The final verse is characterized by a thicker instrumental texture, as the moog synthesizer becomes a viable part of the ensemble. A somewhat uncharacteristic repeat of the A section is enlivened by a dialogue that takes place between the Moog and 3-part vocal chorus. The synthesizer carries the melodic line from the verses while the voices answer with a development of the upper motive from measures 13 and 23. This wordless ululation in the concluding measures suggests that the wonders beheld by the poet are beyond the expressive powers of discursive language.

STEP SEVEN—ONTO-HISTORICAL WORLDS

The music of the Beatles presents the analyst with a series of difficulties regarding paradigmatic focus. For instance, this study places a high premium on an assumed classicism inherent in the *Abbey Road* medley. But while one is busy uncovering evidence that tends to support such a view, one is confronted with musical elements that seem more characteristic of a postmodern aesthetic that is fundamentally hostile to the classical notion of organic unity.

In *The Beatles with Lacan*, Henry W. Sullivan offers an elegant solution to this dilemma by characterizing the group as high priests symbolically presiding over a funeral for the Modern Era (1500–1950). He goes on to describe their unique role in Western culture as part of a celebration of the old (modernist) that was simultaneously involved in an engagement of the new (postmodernist).[17] The process he describes is evident in the track "Because," in which various musical elements combine to create a dialectic between modernist and postmodernist aesthetics.

The choice of a harpsichord as the primary instrument establishes an audible link with the baroque and pre-classical eras. The Beatles then choose to double the harpsichord with an electric guitar, an instrument that is predicated for its very existence on the development of technology in the postmodern era.

Example 10.   Prelude "Because"—Harpsichord and Electric Guitar

This process of integration and synthesis between the two eras continues in the distinctive three-part harmony vocals that constitute the melodic line of "Because." As previously noted, the three-part vocal harmony was recorded a total of three times in order to achieve the effect of a nine-voice choir. While rooted in traditional methods of orchestration, this technique of layering the same voice over a series of different tracks is only possible with the advent of multitrack recording.

Example 11.   Prelude "Because"—Vocal Harmony

Additionally, the hushed quality of the vocal parts, a result of close-miking techniques, allows the singers to intimately engage the listener while at the same time maintaining a full choral texture.

Finally, the use of the Moog synthesizer is perhaps the clearest indication of an integration of modernist and postmodernist aesthetic stances. Developed in early 1964 by Robert Moog, this instrument was initially celebrated for its ability to produce exotic sounds that were primarily employed for their novel effect on a variety of popular recordings.[18] In fact; the otherworldly quality of these sounds was the instrument's primary selling point. Even more than the electric guitar, the synthesizer is an instrument that depends on modern technology for its very existence. The Beatles, however, chose to use the Moog in a way that thwarts conventional expectations. On "Because," the band seems to be focused more on the instrument's timbral potential and proceeds to incorporate it into the ensemble.

The Moog first enters at measure 31 by doubling the harpsichord and guitar lines. It thereby thickens the musical texture, while at the same time grounding the text's emphasis on the interpersonal.

Example 12.   Prelude "Because"—Entrance of Moog (m. 31)

The Moog's next entrance is at measure 45 where it restates the melody by using what seems to be a saw-tooth waveform. Strangely suggestive of a pastoral setting, the use of the synthesizer in this passage displays a traditional approach to instrumentation within the context of a technology that was state of the art for its time.

Through the skillful manipulation of the aforementioned musical elements, "Because" successfully conveys the experiences of an everyman living in Western culture in the late twentieth century. Poised as he was within the transition between two aesthetic paradigms (modernist and postmodernist), this everyman was a creature firmly rooted in a philosophical mindset that valued structural unity. At the same time, he was confronted by an emerging technology that portrayed the world in terms of a dizzying mosaic in which all attempts at thematic reduction seemed utterly hopeless. As two life-worlds collided, there was a yearning for simplicity—a return to the garden. "Because" offers that return but the garden it presents is a place where more questions are raised than are ultimately answered.

Example 13. Prelude "Because"—Moog Solo

STEP EIGHT—OPEN LISTENING

The slow tempo reported in the first open listening now has deeper ramifications. It is a soothing but strangely disconcerting pattern that seems to lead one toward the stillness of mind necessary for a proper engagement of the issues raised by the text. The entrance of the vocal harmony is magical and seems to deliver the nirvana promised by the rigid adherence to structure observed in the introduction. The gradual thickening of texture that is triggered by the entrance of the Moog synthesizer begins a noticeable process of intensification within the work and also introduces a palpable anxiety that is engendered by the philosophical inquiry given voice in the text.

The second open listening makes it clear that "Because" is a response to a query that was raised before the track began. The unheard question Why? is implicit in the imagery of the text, as well as in the music's persistent forward motion. Ultimately, however, there is a resignation to the idea that the original question was unanswerable. Despite this, one is not left with a sense of despair, but rather, a lingering sense of mystery.

STEP NINE—META-CRITIQUE

The preceding analysis has generated a wealth of useful data concerning the song "Because," that, within the context of this study, is considered as the prelude to the *Abbey Road* medley. The chosen method (eclectic) has allowed the analyst the opportunity to view the work from a variety of perspectives so as not to miss relevant information that might fall beyond the scope of any particular analytical approach. As one moves through the analysis, one senses a dimensionality in the work not readily apparent from any individual aesthetic stance. As a result, it became possible to gain a deeper understanding of the work's true significance.

The greatest strength of the preceding analysis was its attempt to incorporate discussions of recording technique into the analysis of musical form. Combined with the phenomenological descriptions presented in step four (the sound-in-time), these discussions helped foreground the essential qualities of the music as pure sound. Since such qualities lie beyond the scope of formal methods—but are crucial to an informed understanding of a recorded work—subsequent chapters will continue to attempt this challenging but necessary synthesis.

NOTES

1. Mark Lewisohn, *The Beatles' Recording Sessions* (New York: Harmony Books, 1988), 184–85.

2. Lewisohn, *Recording Sessions*, 187.

3. Terence J. O'Grady, *The Beatles: A Musical Evolution* (Boston: Twayne Publishers, 1983), 161–62.

4. Ian MacDonald, *Revolution in the Head: The Beatles' Records and the Sixties* (New York: H. Holt, 1994), 291–92.

5. Lewisohn, *Recording Sessions*, 72.

6. MacDonald, *Revolution in the Head*, 261.

7. MacDonald, *Revolution in the Head*, 234.

8. This, and all subsequent musical examples from the *Abbey Road* medley are derived from a full-score transcription created by the author. This transcription was based on two sources: *The Beatles: Complete Scores* (1993) and Walter Everett's *The Beatles as Musicians:* Revolver *Through* The Anthology (New York: Oxford University Press, 1999). The results were then checked against the actual recordings, in order to modify any possible errors and to transcribe the brass and string orchestrations for which no definitive score currently exists.

9. Everett, *The Beatles as Musicians:* Revolver *Through* The Anthology, 259.

10. Everett, *The Beatles as Musicians:* Revolver *Through* The Anthology, 259.

11. It is interesting to consider that the elaborate overdubbing evident on the *Sgt. Pepper's* track, "A Day in the Life," was actually achieved by the synchronization of two 4-track recorders.

12. Lewisohn, *Recording Sessions*, 153.

13. Lewisohn, *Recording Sessions*, 184.

14. Andy Babiuk, *The Beatles' Gear: All the Fab Four's Instruments from Stage to Studio* (San Francisco: Backbeat Books, 2001), 247.

15. Lewisohn, *Recording Sessions*, 185.

16. Ian Hammond, "Because," *Beathoven: Studying the Beatles*, http://www.geocities.com/hammodotcom/beathoven/because1.htm (July 15, 2007). In an article on his website focusing on the song "Because," Hammond points out the causal relationships at work within the lyric.

17. Henry W. Sullivan, *The Beatles with Lacan: Rock 'n' Roll as Requiem for the Modern Age* (New York: P. Lang, 1995), 153–70.

18. Stanley Sadie, ed., *The New Grove Dictionary of Music and Musicians, Second Edition, Volume Seventeen* (New York: Thames & Hudson, 2001), 75–76.

5

MOVEMENT I: "YOU NEVER GIVE ME YOUR MONEY"/"OUT OF COLLEGE"/"ONE SWEET DREAM"

STEP ONE—HISTORICAL BACKGROUND

Within the context of this study, "You Never Give Me Your Money" is considered as Movement I of the *Abbey Road* medley. According to the session notes documented by Mark Lewisohn, this was the first recording specifically intended for the *Abbey Road* medley. The basic tracks were recorded at Olympic Studios on May 6, 1969. Subsequent recording, overdubbing, and mixing sessions took place at Abbey Road on July 1, 15, 30, and 31 and August 5, 13, 14, and 21, 1969.[1]

Largely the work of composer Paul McCartney, this is only the second example of a through-composed work in the Beatles' entire catalog. The first, Lennon's "Happiness Is a Warm Gun," consisted of four contrasting sections and was recorded during sessions for *The Beatles* (LP) (1968). Following Lennon's archetype, McCartney presents three sections in less than four minutes, thereby demonstrating a thorough mastery of musical form and genre.

Generally thought to be a guarded and somewhat spiteful lament for the fragmenting business relationships within the group,[2] "You Never Give Me Your Money" ultimately generates a remarkable emotional resonance. In its opening section, the singer's regret sets off a chain of reminiscences concerning the Beatles' long and winding journey between

1962 and 1970. As such, it can be viewed as a major arrival point for the group in terms of lyrical as well as musical content.

The origins of the medley as an extended work flowing for almost the entire side of an album are generally attributed to composer Paul McCartney and producer George Martin.[3] Although McCartney has had little to say on the subject, Martin has tended to confirm the view that John Lennon was fundamentally opposed to the idea of extended form. As the sessions neared completion, Lennon is reputed to have demanded that all of his songs be on one side of the record while all of Paul's be on the other.[4]

There is, however, an intriguing account that tends to contradict this view. In an interview given to *New Musical Express* in April 1969, Lennon said, "Paul and I are now working on a kind of song montage that we might do as one piece on one side. We've got about two weeks to finish the whole thing, so we're really working at it."[5] The fact that the recording of the basic tracks of Movement I ("You Never Give Me Your Money") began on May 6, 1969, seems to validate Lennon's somewhat obscure comment—and emphasizes how *both* composers were under pressure to prepare the material for the medley in order to meet the deadline of upcoming recording dates.

STEP TWO—OPEN LISTENINGS

The work is performed in a slow tempo. The introduction, which is played plaintively on piano suggests a synthesis of the secular and the sacred—that is, a solemn, reverential approach in the musical accompaniment that contrasts sharply with a text that focuses on matters of friendship and finance. At 00:09 (measure 4), the entrance of the electric guitar creates a remarkable aural effect.

Example 14.   Movement I—Entrance of Electric Guitar

The question of what instrument is actually playing here remains an open one. The part could easily be mistaken for an electric bass since the opening notes are played predominantly in a range that corresponds to the electric guitar's middle and lower registers.[6] The vocal line then enters and moves in tandem with the piano. At 0:32, the melody is double-tracked on the words "funny paper." This effect suggests an aural depth to the recording that was not previously apparent. At 0:41, the double-tracking effect is repeated on the words "break down." The opening phrase is then restated at measure 17, this time in three-part harmony.

Following a one-measure cadence, the work segues directly into Section B: That Magic Feeling. This section is characterized by a jaunty barrelhouse texture in which the predominant instrument is a piano that plays syncopated lines in boogie-woogie style against the main melody. Over this pattern, a husky vocal by McCartney presents a description of youthful abandon that remains hopeful despite limited personal prospects.

> Out of college, money spent
> See no future, pay no rent
> All the money's gone, nowhere to go
> Any jobber got the sack
> Monday morning, turning back
> Yellow lorry slow, nowhere to go
> But, oh that magic feeling,
> Nowhere to go

The final line, "Oh, that magic feeling, nowhere to go," introduces a change in the textural fabric, as electric guitar arpeggios create an aural backdrop for three-part harmony vocals in the style of Prelude "Because." Within this texture, a second electric guitar improvises freely in the middle to lower registers over a modified double-plagal cadence.[7] This pattern then develops into a climbing transition that elaborates a diminished seventh chord. The transition then leads triumphantly into a new section, which is characterized by the first contemporary groove heard thus far. As a chugging electric guitar drives the song forward, the vocalist extols the pleasures of a younger, more carefree existence. Soon however, the lyric describes a sense of underlying pain or grief with the following lines:

> Soon we'll be away from here
> Step on the gas and wipe that tear away

Here, the music provides an appropriate setting for the shift in mood as the minor subdominant harmony moves in a syncopated passing-tone pattern in inversion. The music then moves once again into a modified cadence, which supports a nursery-rhyme lyric in three-part harmony that seems to bid a sad farewell to childish things:

> One two three four five six seven,
> All good children go to Heaven

STEP THREE—MUSICAL SYNTAX

Key: a minor / C Major / A Major
Meter: 4/4
Form: Through-composed ‖ A ‖ B ‖ C ‖
   "You Never Give Me Your Money" is a through-composed work in which none of the three distinct sections are repeated. The song opens in the key of A minor but moves quickly to C major for Section B. Thereafter, new material is introduced in the key of A major by means of an octatonic transition played on electric guitar. This transition leads to a coda that consists of a repeating cadence that incorporates harmonic elements common to both A major and C major. Example 15 presents a harmonic reduction of Movement I that highlights the transitions between different sections.
   In its frequent alternation of tonal centers built on A and C, Movement I seems to portend the structural layout of the entire medley. Oppositions established here reach their greatest tension in Movement II and their ultimate resolution at the conclusion of Movement III. In *Beethoven, Tristan, and the Beatles* (1990), theorist Robert Gauldin describes this intriguing compositional strategy:

> In comparison to most rock albums of that period, the tonal organization of the second side of *Abbey Road* is nothing less than astounding. One

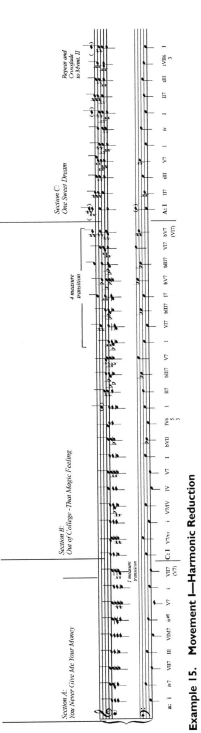

Example 15. Movement I—Harmonic Reduction

strongly suspects that George Martin may have ultimately been responsible for the structure of this series of songs, some of which are apparently
former rejects. Be that as it may, what I find most intriguing is the tonal
conflict created by the struggle for control between the two chief protagonists of A and C.[8]

Movement I's "You Never Give Me Your Money" is a lament that contains elements of what author Terence O'Grady refers to as the "adult
commercial ballad." In his book, O'Grady describes this genre with regard to the song "Yesterday" (1965):

> "Yesterday" is not exclusively an adult commercial ballad; it shows char-
> acteristics associated with the rock ballad and pop-rock styles as well. The
> prominent use of the vi-V-IV progression in the bridge (suggested also in
> measures 3 and 4 of the verse) is typical of rock ballads in general, while
> the unexpected chromatic mediant relationship found between measures
> 7 and 8 is especially typical of earlier Beatle pop-rock songs (i.e., vi-II7-
> IV-I). "Yesterday," therefore, is a synthesis of the adult commercial ballad
> style, the rock ballad, and the pop-rock style.[9]

In a similar manner, "You Never Give Me Your Money" fuses folk-ballad
style with musical elements more commonly associated with popular jazz
standards. This characteristic is particularly evident at the cadences in
mm. 6–7, mm. 14–15, and mm. 22–23, which employ half-diminished
seventh chords built on the supertonic, in a predominant function.

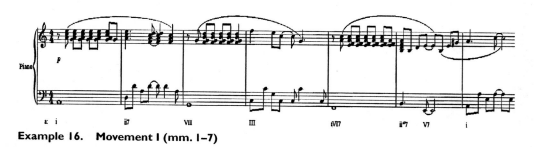

Example 16.   Movement I (mm. 1–7)

As the singer expresses regret at the loss of intimacy with a loved
one, the melodic line hangs precariously on the fifth degree of the
scale. Gradually, the vocalist initiates a reluctant descent to the tonic
perhaps suggesting resignation to the inevitable breakdown of a long-
term relationship.

Example 17.   Movement I—Melodic Line (Section A)

In Section B, the first actual harmonic modulation is implemented, this time to the relative major. The melody of the first half of this section is active and jaunty and, along with the lyric, evokes the early days of the relationship described in the opening sequence.[10] The melodic line that constitutes the main thematic material of the first part of Section B is centered, as was Section A around E5. But now, within the context of the new key area (C major), this pitch is heard as the third degree of the tonic triad.

Example 18.   Movement I—Melodic Line (Section B)

This section initiates a move toward the sub-dominant of the new key (C major) by introducing a modified double-plagal cadence, which is then repeated for thirteen measures as the ground for a three-part vocal harmony reminiscent of the one heard previously in Prelude "Because." In its reiteration of the subtonic triad within the context of the double-plagal cadence, Section B serves to destabilize the tonal center of C major asserted at the end of Section A. It thereby paves the way for the harmonic development of the next section, which is prepared by a transitional bridge of remarkable ingenuity.

The bridge passage that serves as the link between Section B: "Out of College"/"That Magic Feeling" and Section C: "One Sweet Dream" consists of a brief statement of the section's primary motive, which is then followed by a succession of diminished seventh chords in support of a climbing melodic pattern that employs elements of the octatonic scale.

Example 19.   Movement I—Melodic Line (Bridge Passage)

The essential contour of this passage suggests an allusion to measures 55–56 of George Gershwin's *Rhapsody in Blue*.[11] But the differences between the two motives are as intriguing as their similarities.

Example 20.   *Rhapsody In Blue* (mm. 55–56)[12]

Note that whereas Gershwin features a melodic ninth over a dominant seventh (suggesting a half-diminished seventh chord), the Beatles choose to employ the enharmonic equivalent of a flatted ninth thereby creating the effect of a fully diminished seventh chord. Additionally, the rhythmic structure in the Gershwin example is relatively straightforward, whereas the Beatles choose to employ a syncopated harmonic strategy throughout.

Following the transitional bridge passage, the arrival of Section C places Movement I firmly in the key of A major. The guitar accompaniment forms a harmonic and rhythmic bed for the elemental melodic line, which articulates the interval of an octave. Soon, however, modal mixture is reintroduced as the progression moves from B7 (V/V) to a bIII that is employed here in a predominant function (I–II–bIII–V–I). As well as expanding the expressive scope of Section C, this chord usage serves to foreground the aforementioned compositional strategy (double-tonic) and also points the way toward further structural development to come. The subsequent appearance of the minor subdominant (iv) completes the process. Following a brief restatement of the opening material of Section C, the first movement comes to an ambiguous close with a repeating nursery rhyme sung over a descending harmonic progression (bIII–bVII⁶–I) that incorporates elements of the aforementioned double-tonic structure.

In its articulation of the interval of an octave, the melodic material of Section C exhibits the clearest emphasis of a tonal center, in this case A, of any of the three sections of Movement I. The opening leap of a minor sixth (C# to A) simultaneously emphasizes the tonic (A), and its quality (major). This is followed by a reiteration of scale degree 5.

Example 21. Movement I—Melody and Accompaniment (Bridge Passage)

One sweet   dream___   pick up the bags and get   in the lim − o − sine.___

Example 22.   Movement I—Melodic Line (mm. 54–56)

The remaining thematic material reflects the mode mixture of the harmonic structure by including elements of A minor and C major in mm. 58–59. This is followed by a restatement of the melody heard in mm. 54–56, now modified to accommodate the descending progression that concludes Movement I.

Final Thoughts: Musical Syntax

In Movement I, the process of mode mixture possesses a double function. On the surface, it expands the music's expressive power by means of a mutation of the primary harmonic material. However, since the work itself seems built on a dialectical relationship between the key areas of A and C, the mixture technique also facilitates a structural prolongation that necessitates further tonal development in subsequent movements. Thus, mode mixture is ultimately revealed as the means for articulating a large-scale tonal structure. The work derives much of its forward momentum from this ingenious compositional strategy.

Additionally, the genre mixing that is an ever-increasing characteristic of late-period Beatles music is most pronounced in Section A. Here, jazz-based harmonies common to popular standards are effectively integrated into a folk-ballad style. This blending seems to parallel the harmonic strategy of mode mixture that increases in Sections B and C and also serves to emphasize the work's eclectic character.

RECORDING STRATEGIES

As previously mentioned in the analysis of Prelude "Because" in chapter 4, the introduction of 8-track techniques in Beatles recordings in

1968 meant that the group no longer had to limit their arrangements and production ideas to save space on the master tape. This resulted in fewer reduction mixes, and consequently the arrangements on *Abbey Road* are more varied and complex than on any of the group's previous recordings.

An additional point of interest is the fact that until *Abbey Road* all Beatles albums were released in both mono and stereo. During the late period (1967–1969), group members were only directly involved in the mono mix. Producer George Martin and various EMI engineers would typically create the stereo mixes for albums such as *Sgt. Pepper's Lonely Hearts Club Band* (1967), *Magical Mystery Tour* (1967), and *The Beatles* (1968) at a later date.[13] Consequently, the differences between the stereo and mono mixes of late-period Beatles albums are often quite striking. Since the end results differ so noticeably from track to track, an argument could be made that these alternate mixes actually constitute entirely different works.

In the case of *Abbey Road*, however, no mono mix was issued in either America or the UK.[14] The album thus differs from earlier Beatles works in that it is a stereo conception from start to finish. This quality is particularly evident throughout Movement I, which features excessive stereo panning combined with an eccentric approach to instrumentation. Evidence suggests that the Beatles were keenly interested in the aesthetic possibilities inherent in stereo mixing.

STEP FOUR—THE SOUND-IN-TIME

Out of the silence, which seems intensified by the unresolved harmonic entity of the previous track (Prelude "Because"), a piano enters on the left channel with a soothing eighth-note pattern in the middle register. At 0:09, an electric guitar(?) enters on the right channel, making a subtle commentary on the melody evident in the uppermost part of the piano line. At 0:23, a solo vocal enters invoking the title line ("You Never Give Me Your Money"). The voice is soft, supple, and mournful in tone. At 0:32, vocal double-tracking occurs on the line "funny paper." This doubling continues through to the end of the first verse. At 0:47, the doubled vocal expands into a three-part harmony. A gentle cymbal part enters on the right channel and continues through the end of verse 2, at which point a rich reverberation is heard on the vocal track. Following a brief transition, a new section begins at 1:10.

Things now divide markedly across the stereo spectrum. A prominent honky-tonk piano line and bass guitar are featured on the left channel, while an effect-laden vocal backed by drums and percussion is heard on the right. At 1:31, a chiming electric guitar enters on the left channel in conjunction with a general slowing down of the harmonic rhythm. At 1:48, an angelic chorus enters in the center in addition to a mid-register electric guitar solo on the right channel. At 2:09, two more electric guitars appear on the left and right side of the stereo image. Together, they sound a rising melodic line that gradually increases in dynamic intensity before concluding at 2:28.

Next, the singer returns in the center of the aural image intoning a leaping melodic line near the top of his vocal register. Electric guitars continue on the left and right channels, subtly commenting on the melodic material. At 2:47, the guitars begin to sound a chiming line, which repeatedly descends under the lead vocal, before ascending triumphantly on the word "today!" At 3:01, the singer begins to improvise freely in the upper register while one of the electric guitars begins a new line on the right channel. An unusually active electric bass echoes the ascending guitar line heard earlier and concludes with a flourish of rapidly plucked notes.

At 3:09, a chorus of singers enters with what seems to be a fragment from an obscure nursery rhyme. Voices and instruments continue to move and swirl around the stereo spectrum before melding into an elaborate transition that involves crickets, water sounds, and exotic percussion.

STEP FIVE—MUSICAL AND TEXTUAL REPRESENTATION

You Never Give Me Your Money

> You never give me your money
> You only give me your funny paper
> And in the middle of negotiations
> You break down
> I never give you my number

I only give you my situation
And in the middle of investigation
I break down
Out of college, money spent
See no future, pay no rent
All the money's gone, nowhere to go
Any jobber got the sack
Monday morning, turning back
Yellow lorry slow, nowhere to go
But, oh that magic feeling,
Nowhere to go
Oh, that magic feeling
Nowhere to go
One sweet dream
Pick up the bags and get in the limousine
Soon we'll be away from here
Step on the gas and wipe that tear away
One sweet dream came true today
Came true today
Came true today (yes it did)
One two three four five six seven,
All good children go to Heaven

The Beatles began their career with clearly defined personae due mainly to the impact of the film *A Hard Day's Night* (1964). In a script written by playwright Alun Owen, the group members are portrayed as four parts of a collective personality: John Lennon as witty, acerbic, and intellectual; Paul McCartney as outgoing, thoughtful, and personable; George Harrison as skeptical, moody, and self-contained; and Ringo Starr as innocent, unassuming, and kind. Although these "characters" were invented for the film, they were based largely on the screenwriter's personal experiences.[15] On a tour of Great Britain in early 1964, Owen was granted access to the group on a daily basis and thereafter distilled the various traits he observed into highly structured characterizations.[16] In addition to providing *A Hard Day's Night* with a strong narrative center, the reductions in Owen's script seems to have aided the group's compositional process over the next three years. Essentially, it gave each Beatle a theatrical mask through which to express a distinctly personal view.

However, as their career progressed, there emerged a collective weariness with these characterizations and a concomitant attempt to escape their constrictive influence. In *Many Years from Now*, Paul McCartney describes an intriguing compositional strategy employed by the group during the making of the album *Sgt. Pepper's Lonely Hearts Club Band* (1967):

> So I had this idea of giving the Beatles alter egos simply to get a different approach; then when John came up to the microphone or I did, it wouldn't be John or Paul singing, it would be the members of this band. It would be a freeing element. I thought we can run this philosophy through the whole album; with this alter-ego band, it won't be us making all that sound, it won't be the Beatles, it'll be this other band, so we'll be able to lose our identities in this.[17]

The process McCartney describes was evidently a liberating experience since the resulting album was populated by a dazzling array of characters (Lovely Rita, Billy Shears, Mr. Kite, and so on) each with a personal perspective quite distinct from the group's prior narrative voice(s). This trend continued in the film *Magical Mystery Tour* (1967), which presents the Beatles as wizards who act as catalysts for a group of travelers on holiday. On *The White Album* (1968), the new songs range in scope from parodies of the group's own personae (*Mother Nature's Son, Blackbird, I Will*) to bizarre character studies (*The Continuing Story of Bungalow Bill, Sexy Sadie, Rocky Raccoon*) that outdo even the more colorful creations of *Sgt. Pepper*.[18]

These developments suggest an ongoing effort to circumvent the constrictive influence of the group's early image. By the time they arrived at the *Abbey Road* medley, the Beatles had achieved a remarkable anonymity of voice that makes their final work at once biographical and universal.

On the surface level, the text of Section A: "You Never Give Me Your Money" exhibits a preoccupation with long vowel sounds. These vowels are employed in a syntactical structure that focuses on the personal pronouns "me" and "you," thereby foregrounding the extremely intimate nature of this section's overall tone. On a deeper structural level, word meaning is consistently manipulated in an apparent effort to direct the listener's attention to the connections that exist between material gain and personal loss. As a result, the narrator's obsessive interest in finance can be seen as a symbol of permanent estrangement within the context of a personal relationship that is beyond all hope of repair. Following the end of the second verse, the prevailing impression that we are in the present tense is challenged by an abrupt time change in the musical setting that prepares the listener for the fragmented textual structures of Section B.

On the surface level, the text of Section B: "Out of College"/"That Magic Feeling" exhibits a preoccupation with hardness. In contrast with the smooth vowel formations of Section A, the words here tend to end with short, clipped consonants. Additionally, the overall structure seems fragmented as various phrases are strung together in a seemingly random fashion to form an emerging image of events from the past. On a deeper structural level, this fragmentation creates a mosaic that gradually comes together as the listener moves through the work.

In Section C: "One Sweet Dream," the picture begins to come into focus as the fragmented elements that characterized Section B are unified within the context of an emerging narrative structure. The surface of the text exhibits many of the vowel sounds that were a feature of Section A, suggesting perhaps that the narrator is more personally involved in the events being described. At a deeper structural level, the narrative conveys a sense of youthful excitement strangely underscored by a palpable anxiety regarding the contingencies of a rootless, career-driven lifestyle. The final rhyming couplet presents a nursery rhyme cum prayer, which gives emphasis to the anxiety discernible throughout Section C. The listener is thus transported out of the present into a dream-like state that will serve as the narrative setting for Movement II.

STEP SIX—VIRTUAL FEELING

As was seen in the analysis of musical and textual representations, the first movement is largely concerned with temporality in that it addresses present-day concerns and conflicts by placing them within the context of a long-term relationship. The opening phrase, accompanied plaintively on piano, conveys the singer's mournful resignation to the inevitable dissolution of platonic love:

> You never give me your money
> You only give me your funny paper
> And in the middle of negotiations
> You break down

This quality is undermined by the ambiguous nature of the jazz-derived harmonies that appear at structural cadences in Section A. As a result, with reference to the human interaction described in the lyric, one is struck by an implicit conflict at work between the secular and the sacred.

Through what might be described as the musical correlative of a cinematic hard-cut (fore-grounded cadence in the key of the relative major), the narrative moves from the present (actual time in Section A) to the past (historical time in Section B). The use of an overly schematized chord progression (I–V/vi–vi–V/IV–IV–V–I) in the first part of Section B suggests an unreliable first-person narration at work—that is, things seem more comfortably predictable in retrospect than at the time they actually occurred.

> Out of college, money spent
> See no future, pay no rent
> All the money's gone, nowhere to go
> Any jobber got the sack
> Monday morning, turning back
> Yellow lorry slow, nowhere to go

The second part of Section B confirms this notion, since it withdraws from anecdotal renderings to focus instead on the narrator's feelings about the events that are being described:

> But, oh that magic feeling,
> Nowhere to go
> Oh, that magic feeling
> Nowhere to go

The transition is now complete from uphill struggle to the fruits of early success. The melodic leap on the words "One sweet dream" conveys an appropriate sense of release over a harmonic structure that embodies the medley's architectural framework. Section C continues the narrative's focus on past events first presented in the previous section. Following an elaborate bridge, the final section of Movement I offers a detailed description of the rootless lifestyle that characterized the band's early career. The forward propulsion of the music's chugging rhythmic accompaniment suggests that gains in professional momentum were achieved at a high personal price.

The ultimate outcome of these various narrative effects is a suspension of what Susanne K. Langer called clock-time, or the time measured strictly as incremental units.[19] This suspension serves to pave the way for the internally experienced aesthetic time that is evoked at the beginning of Movement II.

STEP SEVEN—ONTO-HISTORICAL WORLDS

As in many examples from Paul McCartney's late-period Beatles output, the narrative structure of Movement I explores the connections that exist between memory and present-day experience. In *Penny Lane* (1967), the narrative established a dialectical relationship between childhood reminiscences and the self-assured stance of young adulthood. In that song, past events are portrayed with great specificity, while present tenses are couched in a metaphorical language rich in subjective allusion. In Movement I of the *Abbey Road* medley, McCartney continues to explore the possibilities of this technique in a less schematic and more fully integrated fashion.

In its use of temporal references, which are increasingly discontinuous as the work progresses, Movement I exhibits nuances that suggest a Proustian journey through experiential time. Gérard Genette writes:

> First of all, we should note the extensive shifts in relative duration, ranging from one line of text for ten years to 190 pages for two to three hours, or from approximately one page per century to one page per minute. . . . As the Proustian narrative moves towards its conclusion, it becomes

increasingly discontinuous, consisting of gigantic scenes separated from each other by enormous gaps. It deviates more and more from the ideal "norm" of an isochronic narrative.[20]

Temporal shifts similar to those described by Genette also seem to be operating in Movement I, as the isochronic narratives typical of pop-rock styles are subtly adapted toward the work's larger purpose. In Section A, the text begins in the present with a mournful lament for the current state of a close relationship.

> You never give me your money
> You only give me your funny paper
> And in the middle of negotiations
> You break down

Then, in Section B, we move abruptly to a decade earlier when the relationship that was the subject of Section A was in its formative stage. Note how the present tenses of Section A have now given way to a fragmented narrative that portrays a temporal state which could last days, months, or even years:

> Out of college, money spent
> See no future, pay no rent
> All the money's gone, nowhere to go
> Any jobber got the sack
> Monday morning, turning back
> Yellow lorry slow, nowhere to go

In the second half of Section B, we return to the present as the narrator comments on a seemingly sweeter, more carefree existence:

> But, oh that magic feeling,
> Nowhere to go
> Oh, that magic feeling
> Nowhere to go

Following an instrumental passage, Section C presents a series of events that lie somewhere between the temporal worlds of Sections A and B.

One sweet dream
Pick up the bags and get in the limousine
Soon we'll be away from here
Step on the gas and wipe that tear away
One sweet dream came true today
Came true today
Came true today (yes it did)

Finally, in the coda, we cut to a time that precedes the events recounted
in Section B. Here, childhood innocence is evoked by a rhyming couplet, which functions simultaneously as nursery rhyme and fervent
prayer:

One two three four five six seven,
All good children go to Heaven

The discontinuous nature of the text of Movement I serves to disrupt
traditional narrative structure in ways that suggest a Proustian approach
to temporality. As such, it conveys the aspirations of a mid-twentieth-
century *lebenswelt* (life-world) in which the inhabitants of Western culture, while in the grips of a paradigmatic shift from modernism to postmodernism, eagerly sought temporal release by means of a heightened
understanding of Eastern philosophy. Paul McCartney described the
nature of these aspirations within the context of his own experience with
transcendental meditation: "For me, then, it was the sixties, I'd been doing a bunch of drugs, I wasn't in love with anyone, I hadn't settled down.
I think maybe I was looking for something to fill some sort of hole. . . .
The whole meditation experience was very good and, I still use the
mantra. . . . I found it very useful and still do."[21] John Lennon elaborated
on this idea, by focusing more exclusively on its cultural relevance: "The
youth of today are really looking for some answers—for proper answers
the established church can't give them, their parents can't give them,
material things can't give them."[22]

In its attempts to expand the parameters of the work beyond the
timebound restrictions of classical narrative, the strategy evident in the
text of Movement I effectively grounds the aspirations of a cultural people, vis-à-vis the search for a level of personal understanding capable of
transcending the conceptual limitations of a passing cultural paradigm.

STEP EIGHT—OPEN LISTENINGS

The work's temporal elements were especially evident during the second series of open listenings. The plaintiveness of the opening section (Section A), which was originally comforting, now exhibits a distinct eeriness as one prepares for the uncharted journey through experiential time. Text and texture draw the listener into the work in a way that now seems irresistible. The tension of the opening section explodes into Section B, which now seems languorous yet inevitable. As we move into the transition to Section C, the past is made remarkably vivid as compared with the detached quality that characterized Section A. The final section (Section C) suggests a yearning for lost innocence, a heartfelt cry from an increasingly disordered present.

STEP NINE—META-CRITIQUE

During the sound-in-time analysis (step four), recognition of the Beatles' seeming fascination with the narrative possibilities engendered by stereo mixing helped foreground the music's suspension of real (actual) time. As a result, one was able to gain a clearer sense of the setting in which the narrative of Movement I unfolds. The dualism implicit in this discussion impacted on the referential analysis of steps five, six, and seven. In particular, the section that focused on onto-historical worlds revealed a Proustian influence on the text and also highlighted the ways in which that influence facilitated an innovative approach to narrative structure.

Arguably, the weakest section of the preceding analysis was the ongoing attempt to incorporate discussions of recording technique into the analysis of musical syntax. Accounts of the Beatles fascination with 8-track recording and stereo mixing were not as compelling as those offered in chapter 4. However, enough flexibility was noted to warrant further attempts in subsequent movements.

NOTES

1. Mark Lewisohn, *The Beatles' Recording Sessions* (New York: Harmony Books, 1988), 176-91.

2. Lewisohn, *Recording Sessions*, 176.

3. Allan Kozinn, *The Beatles* (London: Phaidon, 1995), 201.

4. Lewisohn, *Recording Sessions*, 193.

5. Peter Doggett, *Let It Be/Abbey Road: The Beatles* (New York, London: Schirmer Books/Prentice Hall International, 1998) 49.

6. In *The Beatles' Gear: All the Fab Four's Instruments from Stage to Studio* (2001), author Andy Babiuk points out that during sessions for the album, *Abbey Road* (1969), the Beatles often used a Fender VI six-string bass guitar (245). "The instrument was like a regular six-string guitar but tuned an octave lower." (227) Although documentation concerning the exact attribution of parts in the *Abbey Road* medley is still sketchy, it seems likely that the distinctive line heard at measure 4 of Movement I is actually being played on a Fender VI.

7. One wonders if this part is also being played on a Fender VI six-string bass guitar.

8. Robert Gauldin, "Beethoven, Tristan, and the Beatles." *College Music Symposium* 30 (1990): 151.

9. Terence J. O'Grady, *The Beatles: A Musical Evolution* (Boston: Twayne Publishers, 1983), 76.

10. It is interesting to note that the relationship described here is not necessarily a love affair; the overall treatment suggests that the love described could equally apply to familial bonds or platonic love between close friends. In this sense, the *Abbey Road* medley is consistent in tone with the group's middle- to late-period work in which the love concept was increasingly abstracted from its sexual connotation toward a more philosophical or religious meaning.

11. The likelihood of this motive being a deliberate quotation increases when one considers George Martin's score for "All You Need Is Love," which features allusions to Glenn Miller's "In the Mood," and "Greensleeves." (See Lewisohn, *Recording Sessions*, 120.)

12. George Gershwin, *Rhapsody in Blue: Piano Solo* (New York: New World Music, 1924), 6.

13. Lewisohn, *Recording Sessions*, 108.

14. Lewisohn, *Recording Sessions*, 192

15. *A Hard Day's Night*, directed by Richard Lester, performed by the Beatles, Wilfrid Brimley, and Victor Spinetti (United Artists, 1964).

16. Barry Miles and Paul McCartney, *Many Years from Now* (New York: H. Holt, 1997), 158.

17. Miles and McCartney, *Many Years from Now*, 303–4.

18. Known through popular consensus as *The White Album* (Lewisohn, *Recording Sessions*, 135).

19. Susanne K. Langer, *Feeling and Form: A Theory of Art* (New York: Scribner, 1953), 109.

20. Gerard Genette, "Time and Narrative in *A la recherche du temps perdu*," in *Essentials of the Theory of Fiction*, ed. Michael J. Hoffman and Patrick D. Murphy (Durham and London: Drake University Press, 1988), 278–98.

21. Miles and McCartney, *Many Years from Now*, 396.

22. The Beatles, *Anthology* (San Francisco: Chronicle Books, 2000), 260.

6

MOVEMENT II: "SUN KING"/"MEAN MR. MUSTARD"/"POLYTHENE PAM"/"SHE CAME IN THROUGH THE BATHROOM WINDOW"

STEP ONE—HISTORICAL BACKGROUND

The Beatles recorded the basic tracks for "Sun King" and "Mean Mr. Mustard" on July 24, 1969, while the first sessions for "Polythene Pam" and "She Came in Through the Bathroom Window" took place on July 25, 1969.[1] With the exception of "She Came in Though the Bathroom Window," which was composed by Paul McCartney, the fragments that make up Movement II are largely the work of John Lennon. "Mean Mr. Mustard" and "Polythene Pam" both date from 1968, whereas "Sun King" first appears during the *Get Back* sessions in January of 1969.[2] It is interesting to note that Lennon's contributions form the structural and referential heart of the *Abbey Road* medley, once again challenging the popular notion that he was fundamentally opposed to the idea of extended forms in popular music.

The two sections of Movement II ("Sun King"/"Mean Mr. Mustard" and "Polythene Pam"/"She Came in Through the Bathroom Window") were each recorded as one continuous take with the ultimate intention of joining them together during editing.[3] This fact lends credence to the premise that the *Abbey Road* medley is an extended form, since the players seem to be gearing their performance style toward long-term structural goals.

STEP TWO—OPEN LISTENING

Movement II begins with an elaborate cross-fade from the final moments of Movement I. During this transition, one can hear what seem to be wind chimes moving across the stereo spectrum, suggesting a cool breeze blowing on a warm summer day. These chimes fade down under the gentle chirping of crickets as the music begins. Guitar and bass emerge seemingly from underwater while playing a rising line in the lower part of their registers. The crickets heard earlier continue throughout, thereby suggesting that afternoon has given way to evening. Suddenly, a chord cluster sounds signaling the entrance of the Sun King.

The mood of the previous night section seems enlivened by the entrance of the vocal line in a new key area. Daylight has now brought a sense of peace and security that is heightened by the pastoral setting previously encountered in Prelude "Because." The philosophical questions posed by that track, however, are nowhere to be found in "Sun King." Perhaps there is a sense that they have been answered satisfactorily, since it now seems that all is well. The restatement of the opening section completes the narrative cycle as night returns. Three-part harmony vocals augment the electric guitar and bass, a setup that evokes a playful sense of oneness with all that is natural and good.

Suddenly, we are transported to an urban setting that is decidedly unsettling. Dickensian street scenes create a backdrop for the sinister ramblings of "Mean Mr. Mustard." A rocking, back-and-forth rhythm that suggests the motion of a primitive machine is the musical background for a disturbing yet ultimately amusing character sketch. The narrator who tells us of Mr. Mustard's exploits (sleeping in the park and shaving in the dark) seems rather sinister himself since he audibly revels in the wanton activities he describes. In the second verse, Sister Pam makes her first appearance and is evidently the main character's sole relation. She spends her days working hard and, whenever possible, tries to involve her brother in respectable social interaction. Her efforts are in vain, however, since Mustard invariably makes an embarrassing scene with some obnoxious bit of behavior designed to outrage any onlookers.

As Mr. Mustard's seesaw comes to an abrupt halt, a startling change in rhythm and texture is effected as a lone acoustic guitar introduces the sordid tale of "Polythene Pam." Pam is evidently the female character from the previous section who is now revealed as leading a sordid double life that involves a penchant for polythene bags and cross-dressing.

The track itself is a remarkable example of understatement with regard to the Beatles' approach to instrumentation. Polyrhythmic structures abound, as guitars, bass, and percussion actively comment on one another's rugged performance style. Through it all, however, lead vocals and intricate counter-melodies keep the frivolity firmly in hand. Toward the end of the track, an electric guitar asserts itself in a rudimentary yet powerful solo. Following several aggressive passes at an insistent double-plagal progression, the guitar yields gracefully to the harmony and begins a downward descent to "She Came in Through the Bathroom Window."

The opening chord played by the ensemble introduces the lead vocalist in a manner that is powerful yet somehow reassuring. Building on the innovative instrumentation of "Polythene Pam," the musicians continue to test the limits of groove. Remarkably, the rhythms ebb and flow, bend and crawl, without ever once losing a sense of direction or underlying danceability. The text tells a confusing yet intriguing tale of young love in the middle of the twentieth century. The narrative portrays a world in which people tend to find each other against all odds, in a decidedly nonrational manner. The relationship depicted here will not save either person involved, but it will most certainly change the both of them forever. Changes, in fact, are already in progress. In order to deal with the realization that his lover steals but cannot rob, the main character/narrator tells us that he has resolved to quit the police department and get a steady job, presumably to support their new household in a more respectable manner.

The song ends on an ambiguous note with the lines "Sunday's on the phone till Monday—Tuesday's on the phone to me, oh yeah," simultaneously recalling the bridge of "Lady Madonna" (1968) and the concluding lines of Movement I ("One, two, three, four, five, six, seven—All good children go to heaven").

STEP THREE—MUSICAL SYNTAX

Key: E Major / C Major / E Major / E Major / A Major
Meter: 4/4
Form: Through-composed ‖ A ‖ B ‖ C ‖ D ‖

   Movement II of the *Abbey Road* medley is another through-composed form in which none of the major sections are repeated. However, each individual section is ingeniously structured so as to maintain a strong sense of forward motion. Since the various song fragments were recorded in two sections—(1) "Sun King"/"Mean Mr. Mustard" and (2) "Polythene Pam"/"She Came in Through the Bathroom Window"— the following analysis will approach Movement II in terms of this essential bipartite structure.

   Section A—Sun King—A/B/A
   Section B—Mean Mr. Mustard—A/A
   Section C—Polythene Pam—A/A
   Section D—She Came in Through the Bathroom Window—A/B/A/A/B

As can be seen in the following harmonic reduction (example 23), Movement II focuses on dominant harmony. The movement opens in E major (V of A major) but moves quickly to C major for the main section of "Sun King." Following this section, new lyrical material is introduced over the quarter-note triplet pattern first heard at the end of Section A. Modeled on *Albatross* (1968) by Fleetwood Mac (as was "Don't Let Me Down" from the *Get Back* sessions),[4] "Sun King" exhibits a subtle sophistication that suggests a further refinement of the Beatles' psychedelic approach, while "Mean Mr. Mustard," an apparent parody of music-hall styles, demonstrates Lennon's fondness for a genre usually associated with McCartney.

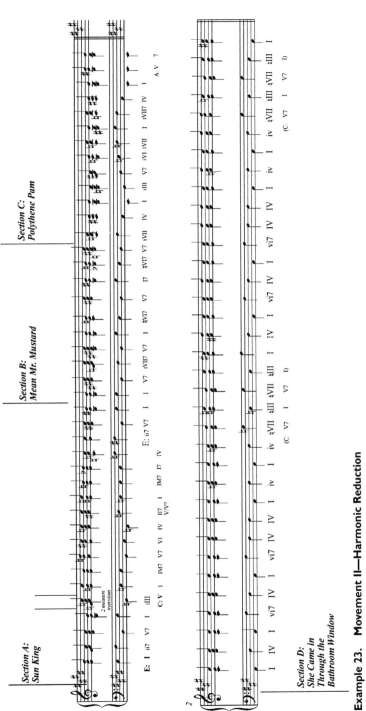

Example 23.   Movement II—Harmonic Reduction

"Polythene Pam" is similar to "Mean Mr. Mustard," but the model has now been updated to feature rock elements notably missing from the previous track. The final section of the movement ("She Came in Through the Bathroom Window") is by McCartney and therefore differs stylistically from the three previous Lennon offerings. Seemingly a return to the stilted rhythmic and textural structures of Movement I, "She Came in Through the Bathroom Window" also plays remarkable games with traditional rock 'n' roll models. Instead of the more typical AABA structure usually associated with rock and pop, the unexpected appearance of another verse at 6:00 suggests a complex ternary structure and thereby lends the work an asymmetry that helps prepare the listener for the more varied structural variations of Movement III.

Part I: "Sun King"/"Mean Mr. Mustard"

Movement II is built on a harmonic structure that alternates two distinct yet related key areas (A and C). Following a transitional interlude between the two movements that, in its use of tape looped sound effects, suggests the influence of *musique concrete*,[5] guitars and bass play a hypnotic riff that stresses scale degree 5 (B natural). Concurrently, the bass drum articulates an intricate rhythmic pattern that features alternations of eighth and sixteenth-note groups neatly echoing elements of the melodic line.

At measure 6, the harmony moves from tonic to supertonic in preparation for the full cadence at mm. 7–8. At measure 17, the tonal focus on E major, which characterized the entire verse of "Sun King," quickly gives way to C major. Following a two-measure transition (mm. 18–19), which articulates an extended dominant harmony in C major, we arrive at the main section of "Sun King."

Firmly planted for the moment in the key of C major, we now have lyrical contrast to the syncopated structures that constituted the bulk of Movement I. A conjunct melodic line is presented here in three parts over a chord pattern that cleverly subverts conventional harmonic function. The V–VI progression in mm. 22–23 seems to operate on the surface as a deceptive cadence, but the VI chord does not sound at all like a part of C major. Rather, it seems to reflect the music's preoccupation with whole-tone relationships. This process continues in mm. 28–31 in

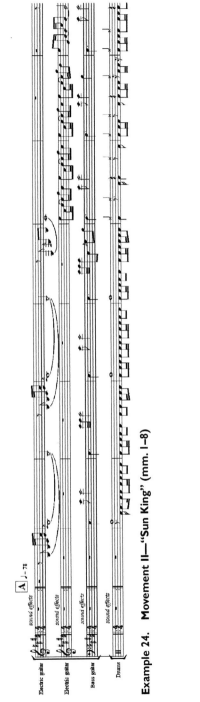

Example 24. Movement II—"Sun King" (mm. 1–8)

Example 25.   Movement II—"Sun King" (mm. 28–31)

which the progression IV–II7 is similarly shifted in order to further
destabilize the tonal center.

   Following a restatement of the material first presented in mm. 20–27,
the harmony slides up chromatically from the subdominant of C (F major) to the supertonic of E major (F# minor). This shift marks the return
of the harmonic material of the introduction.

   The return of the material in E major that constituted the introduction to "Sun King" has now been enhanced with a vocal melody in four-
part harmony that emphasizes a reiterated F# over a repeating ii7–V–I
cadence. Following a full cadence at mm. 46–47, a drum roll introduces
the listener to Section B: "Mean Mr. Mustard."

Example 26.   Movement II—"Sun King" (Outro)

Even more than the previous section, "Mean Mr. Mustard" demonstrates a near-obsession with the key of E major. The opening measures present a seesaw-like rhythmic pattern, which provides the framework for a harmonic structure that focuses on tonic and dominant harmony. Over this foundation, a predominantly triadic melody is presented. This is then followed by a complete restatement of the verse (mm. 48–61) with new text, and the addition of a remarkable vocal harmony in fourths.

Example 27.   Movement II—"Mean Mr. Mustard" (Restatement of A)

The cadence that concluded the first verse (I–bVI–V) is now presented in a metrically modulated form. Originally in 4/4, it now appears in 12/8, an effect that works to ease the transition into the opening of Part II.

Part II: "Polythene Pam"/"She Came in Through the Bathroom Window"

Despite the skill of EMI engineers and producer George Martin, the edit following the final measures of "Mean Mr. Mustard" is clearly audible in both musical and technical terms. As previously noted, the 12/8 rhythm that concluded the previous track helps ease the transition into "Polythene Pam," but the harshness of the edit is still apparent—and perhaps intended.

The track begins with an aggressive double-plagal cadence on acoustic guitar (D-A-E) that affirms the song's tonal center (E major). Especially interesting is Lennon's decision to let the low E string on his guitar ring through every chord in the sequence (D/E–A/E–E). The E thus functions as a tonic pedal and further asserts the song's decisive tonal focus. In spite of these features, "Polythene Pam" is not a simple restatement of the E major harmonic material just presented in "Mean Mr. Mustard." Mode mixture appears halfway through the first verse as Lennon harmonizes his stepwise melody with chords borrowed from the key of C major.

Following a satirical restatement of the bVI–bVII–I cadence *(Yeah, Yeah, Yeah!)* that wryly quotes the Beatles earlier hit, "She Loves You" (1963), the opening chord sequence reappears with an additional instrumental coda built on the same repeating double-plagal harmonic progression (D/E–A/E–E). Over this harmonic structure, an electric guitar solos freely. At measure 121, the progression settles on an E major chord, which is steadily repeated in order to emphasize its gradually emerging function as the dominant of A major, the opening chord of "She Came in Through the Bathroom Window."

The arrival of "She Came in Through the Bathroom Window" reveals how the E major harmony that was the focus of the previous three tracks is actually, within the larger context of the *Abbey Road* medley, an elaborate preparation for the return of A major. The harmonic structure of the verse focuses on A major with an alternation of tonic and subdominant harmony. The move to the minor subdominant in the chorus section seems at first like a further example of the mode mixture that has been a recurring technique throughout the medley.

Soon, however, the minor subdominant is revealed as a means of briefly tonicizing C major, and can therefore be seen as further evidence of the aforementioned double-tonic complex that constitutes the work's underlying compositional strategy.

The reiteration of the verse at measure 143 is complicated by its further restatement between measures 150 and 156. Taking into account the upcoming reappearance of the chorus, this suggestion of a complex ternary form is the most sophisticated formal pattern of Movement II and it strengthens the notion that "She Came in Through the Bathroom Window" is an important arrival point for the entire work. The final appearance of the chorus is a complete restatement of the material first heard in mm. 135–42. However, the final cadence in A major is significant in that it provides a powerful link with the opening measures of Movement III, which are built on A minor.

Example 28. Movement II—"She Came in Through the Bathroom Window" (B Section)

Example 29. Movement II—"She Came in Through the Bathroom Window" (Coda)

Final Thoughts—Musical Syntax

The frequent borrowing of chords from the parallel mode, first seen in Movement I, continues in Movement II. Significantly, this technique is relatively sparse in "Sun King" and "Mean Mr. Mustard" but becomes more frequent in "Polythene Pam" and "She Came in Through the Bathroom Window." With regard to the double-tonic structures described by Robert Gauldin, the early sections of Movement II suggest that for the moment A major has won out.[6] The E major tonality that dominates "Sun King" and "Mean Mr. Mustard" can be considered as an elaboration on the dominant harmony of A major. In particular, the underlying harmonic framework of "Sun King" (E major–C major–E major) suggests that one side of the double-tonic complex is being firmly hemmed in by the dominant of A. The next track, "Mean Mr. Mustard," does little to dissuade the listener of this notion. "Polythene Pam," however, begins to reset the balance as it introduces chordal entities more commonly associated with C major. This process continues in "She Came in Through the Bathroom Window" in which the two keys of the complex (A and C) function respectively as verse and chorus within the same song.

Recording Strategies—Alternate Edits and the Music of Chance

The mixing sessions for Movement II were more elaborate than for any of the other sections of the *Abbey Road* medley. Interestingly, a significant aspect of this process lends credence to the notion that the Beatles were actively employing recording technique as a part of the compositional process. It seems that the album's final track ("Postlude"/"Her Majesty") was originally intended as a midpoint between the two halves of Movement II. Upon hearing the song's placement within the movement, and presumably reacting to the song's tendency to stop forward tonal motion, composer Paul McCartney decided that it wasn't needed and asked engineer John Kurlander to dispose of it. Reluctant to consign any Beatles material to the waste bin, the engineer proceeded to splice the song onto the end of the master reel, separating it from the end of Movement III with leader tape. At a subsequent listening session, when "Her Majesty" serendipitously appeared at the end of the sequence, the group liked the effect so much that they decided to keep it as the medley's concluding track.[7]

The opening chord of "Her Majesty," a D-major triad played by a full rock ensemble, is in fact the final chord of "Mean Mr. Mustard."[8] Example 30 shows the relevant section from the original sequence. While the placement of the tune superficially fits the edit, its tonal center (D major) seems to weigh the aforementioned tonal struggle too strongly in favor of A major.[9] The ultimate effect is that of a suspension of tonal drive in which the forward motion of the medley is abruptly halted.

Example 30.   Movement II—Transcription of Alternate Edit That Features "Her Majesty"

What is evident from the alternate version of Movement II is that the band is actively employing recording technique as a part of the compositional process. As a result, the final version of the medley seems to have as much to do with the recording process as it does with traditional methods of composition. In that sense, its creation could properly be termed, *composing to tape*.[10]

STEP FOUR—THE SOUND-IN-TIME

Out of an evening soundscape replete with crickets and an audibly gentle breeze, a gradually emerging gong, sounding in slow motion, paves the way for the entrance of guitar, bass, and drums at 0:05. This entrance is primarily on the left channel but moves steadily to the center as the music progresses. At 0:57, everything stops as vocal harmonies, which recall prominent elements from Prelude "Because," enter in the center of the stereo spectrum.

At 1:03, the first verse begins. The melody is slow and undulating, full of sustained breathy harmonies that resonate with the gentle strumming of the rhythm guitars. At 1:54, there is an upward shift into a new key area as the vocal harmonies become more insistent. At 2:31, the drums signal the beginning of a new section and activate the work with a new rhythmic structure. The clumsy back and forth motion of the music seems to have comic implications with regard to the song's main character, Mean Mr. Mustard. The bass guitar on the left channel is overdriven to the point of distortion. Following a rhythmic shift at 3:30 that throws the already fragile groove decidedly off-kilter, the section comes to a sudden stop at 3:37, as a stabbing acoustic guitar in the center of the stereo spectrum asserts the beginning of "Polythene Pam."

This new section moves with greater rhythmic urgency. Drums, bass, guitar, and vocals exhibit a random quality that seems to slide across the essential groove of the work. At 4:26, the guitar steps up for an extended solo over an insistent reiteration of the opening chordal riff. At 4:50, the solo concludes as the music begins a measured descent into the next section. At 4:56, the ensemble lands together on the first chord of "She Came in Through the Bathroom Window." The vocalist emerges from the sustained harmony with a warm quality that seems to dissipate the increasing tension of the previous section. The groove is still insistent but far less manic. A sense of relaxed confidence seems to emanate from the ensemble as the musical narrative continues to unfold. At 6:42, the music comes to a stop on an ambiguous harmony, suggesting that there is more development yet to come.

STEP FIVE—MUSICAL AND TEXTUAL REPRESENTATION

Sun King

Here comes the sun king
Here comes the sun king
Everybody's laughing
Everybody's happy
Here comes the sun king.

Quando paramucho mi amore de felice carathon
Mundo paparazzi mi amore cicce erdi parasol
Cuesto abrigado tantamucho que canite carousel

Mean Mr. Mustard

Mean Mr. Mustard sleeps in the park
Shaves in the dark trying to save paper
Sleeps in a hole in the road
Saving up to buy some clothes
Keeps a ten-bob note up his nose
Such a mean old man
Such a mean old man.

His sister Pam works in a shop
She never stops, she's a go-getter
Takes him out to look at the queen
Only place that he's ever been
Always shouts out something obscene
Such a dirty old man
Dirty old man

Polythene Pam

Well you should see Polythene Pam
She's so good-looking but she looks like a man
Well you should see her in drag dressed in her polythene bag
Yes you should see Polythene Pam.
Yeah yeah yeah.

Get a dose of her in jackboots and kilt
She's killer-diller when she's dressed to the hilt
She's the kind of a girl that makes the "News of the World"
Yes you could say she was attractively built.
Yeah yeah yeah.

She Came in Through the Bathroom Window

She came in through the bathroom window
Protected by a silver spoon
But now she sucks her thumb and wonders
By the banks of her own lagoon.

Didn't anybody tell her?
Didn't anybody see?
Sunday's on the phone to Monday,
Tuesday's on the phone to me.

She said she'd always been a dancer
She worked at fifteen clubs a day
And though she thought I knew the answer
Well I knew what I could not say.

And so I quit the police department
And got myself a steady job
And though she tried her best to help me
She could steal but she could not rob.

Didn't anybody tell her?
Didn't anybody see?
Sunday's on the phone to Monday,
Tuesday's on the phone to me
Oh yeah.

In its seemingly random, somewhat disjointed text, Movement II suggests a return to the colorful scenes depicted in *Sgt. Pepper's Lonely Hearts Club Band* (1967) and *Magical Mystery Tour* (1967). The peaceful skies of "Sun King" recall the kaleidoscopic pastures of "Lucy in the Sky with Diamonds," which are now informed by the philosophically charged landscapes depicted in Prelude "Because." As in that work, however, all is not well, for around the corner we encounter the pathological drifter, Mean Mr. Mustard, and the trendy fetishist, Polythene Pam. In its gleeful depiction of the dark side of escapism, Movement II stresses the need for the tonal resolution that will be offered up in Movement III.

On the surface of the text, one finds a descriptive rendering of various aspects of the human condition in Western culture. Employing an unusually high number of extended vowel sounds, Lennon's text paints a dream of placid colors set during the reign of Louis XIV, the Sun King of France (1643–1715).[11] The dream takes place against an idealistic landscape in which Enlightenment promises seem largely fulfilled. Suddenly, there's a shift to the hard consonants of urban life where Mean Mr. Mustard engages in bawdy mischief calculated to subvert a fragile social order. In "Polythene Pam," the naughtiness is now turned inward as perverse fetishes occupy the life of a character that seems to view self-destruction as a viable means of protest. Finally, we are presented with McCartney's "She Came in Through the Bathroom Window" and a text that combines hard consonants and soft vowel sounds in an apparent attempt to make sense of the confusing paradoxes of modern love.

Beneath the surface of the text, one senses a subtle commentary on the historical development of the musicians themselves. "Sun King" recalls the pastoral settings of Strawberry Fields, a Liverpool Salvation Army Home garden where the young John Lennon would spend many happy hours communing with nature and developing his distinctive aesthetic stance.[12] "Mean Mr. Mustard" evokes the early mischievous behavior of group members as they approached young adulthood.[13] "Polythene Pam" creates a portrait of the exotic sex the Beatles encountered on their visits to the notorious seaport of Hamburg, Germany, in the early 1960s.[14] Finally, in "She Came in Through the Bathroom

Window" weary band members struggle to create a viable personal life in the wake of the disruptive influences of wealth and fame.

STEP SIX—VIRTUAL FEELING

As the work opens, one finds sweet relief from the confusion embodied in the final moments of Movement I. Measured guitar and percussion figures reassure the listener with a logic and regularity that seems born of the natural order. Suddenly, a shift in key suggests the arrival of a heavenly vision. Logic and regularity return in the new tonal landscape with the added benefit of the tender mercies of divine providence.

The opening chords of "Mean Mr. Mustard" present a sharp contrast to the ebb and flow rhythms of "Sun King." The machine-like groove suggests the dark and indifferent side of a clockwork universe, in which human suffering bears little or no relevance. The sweet vocal harmony in the second verse and the triplet variations offered in the final cadence offer some relief but ultimately seem more like grudging concessions than true affirmations.

The aggressive guitar chords of "Polythene Pam" seem to strike back at the mechanized rhythms of the previous song. The vocal counter-melodies and elaborate drumming patterns that appear throughout the track attempt to reassert the organic qualities of "Sun King," while simultaneously striking a blow for the human spirit. Although these qualities remain largely on the surface in "Polythene Pam," they are thoroughly integrated in the song that follows.

"She Came in Through the Bathroom Window" creates a sense of resolution regarding the volatile conflicts at work within the previous two tracks. Polyrhythmic patterns and intricate vocal harmonies remain but these elements now seem calmer and more balanced than in either "Mean Mr. Mustard" or "Polythene Pam." One can detect a sense of resignation on the part of the narrator regarding the perplexing events depicted in the lyric.

It is perhaps significant that the musical setting here constitutes the most balanced presentation of the aforementioned competing key areas (A and C) since the conclusion of Movement I. These musical elements could therefore be seen as contributing to the tone and mood of the work in that they seem to resolve the harmonic tension inherent in the first three sections of Movement II.

STEP SEVEN—ONTO-HISTORICAL WORLDS

By means of allegorical imagery and ingenious musical effects, Movement II offers a brief history of Western culture, circa 1700 to 1970. As such, it illuminates the cultural distress engendered by the paradigmatic shift from modernism to postmodernism. In *The Beatles with Lacan*, Henry W. Sullivan described the group's role in this transition by pointing out that "Above all, we have not as yet appreciated their amazing achievement in shepherding our culture out of the decadent sorrows of modernism and into the new, and perhaps frightening unfamiliarity of the postmodern era."[15] The process that Sullivan describes is evident in the narrative structure of Movement II.

Following the blissful landscapes of "Sun King," we are confronted by a new cultural environment that has been fundamentally altered by the pressures of industrialization. The individuals who inhabit this new society (Mean Mr. Mustard and Polythene Pam) have become neurotic and fetishistic perhaps in response to a fragmenting cultural paradigm. In "She Came in Through the Bathroom Window," the narrative lands decisively in the present, resonating with the struggles described by Sullivan regarding the transition from modernism to postmodernism. The characters here seem to exist in a world filled with perplexing contradictions. Presumably, the story concerns a young man and woman who are attempting to find their way through an abstract associational landscape. Despite the evident confusion, they seem able to survive by focusing on the one human element that is common to all historical eras—love.

STEP EIGHT—OPEN LISTENINGS

The suspension of temporal boundaries so important to the narrative development of Movement II was much clearer during the second set of open listenings. Although Movement II is more than two minutes longer than Movement I, it somehow *seems* the same length or shorter.

In addition, the care exhibited by the Beatles and their collaborators regarding the aesthetics of sound recording was especially evident. As previously mentioned, *Abbey Road* was the first album in which the group recorded exclusively in an 8-track format. It was also the only Beatles album released solely in stereo. Remarkably, the challenges engendered by the newly expanded format do not seem to overwhelm the group. On the contrary, they seem to view additional tracks as the means of deepening an already powerful aesthetic stance. A singular quality in the arrangements of Movement II was also noted. Specifically, they seem to defy conventional expectations regarding instrumental formats. Here, the Beatles seem to have been rethinking their templates from the ground up, thereby inventing a new way to play a pop song.

STEP NINE—META-CRITIQUE

The most powerful aspect of the preceding analysis was the incorporation of recording technique into the discussion of musical syntax. The assessment of the alternate sequence of Movement II, which included "Her Majesty" as a midpoint, simultaneously asserted the ingenuity behind the construction of the work and the significance of the group's utilization of recording technique as an integral part of the compositional process.

Conversely, descriptions achieved during the sound-in-time analysis seemed decidedly less powerful than those provided for Prelude/ "Because" or Movement I. Additionally, the onto-historical analysis was somewhat overcomplicated in its attempts to establish a span of three centuries as the basis for a description of this movement's overall narrative structure.

NOTES

1. Mark Lewisohn, *The Beatles' Recording Sessions* (New York: Harmony Books, 1988), 182.

2. Barry Miles and Paul McCartney, *Many Years from Now* (New York: H. Holt, 1997), 556.

3. Lewisohn, *Recording Sessions*, 182.

4. Walter Everett, *The Beatles as Musicians:* Revolver *Through* The Anthology (New York: Oxford University Press, 1999), 263.

5. "*Musique concrète* was created in Paris in 1948 by Pierre Schaeffer (soon joined by Pierre Henry). . . . In *musique concrète* sound materials could be taken from pre-existing recordings (including instrumental and vocal music) and recordings made specially, whether of the environment or with instruments and objects in front of a studio microphone." (Stanley Sadie, ed., *The New Grove Dictionary of Music and Musicians, Second Edition, Volume Eight* (New York: Thames & Hudson, 2001), 60.

6. Robert Gauldin, "Beethoven, Tristan, and the Beatles." *College Music Symposium* 30 (1990): 151.

7. Lewisohn, *Recording Sessions*, 183.

8. Lewisohn, *Recording Sessions*, 183.

9. One could perhaps make the argument that in the alternate edit, "Her Majesty" is functioning like a cadenza, in that it serves to suspend forward temporal and tonal motion. However, one would still have to contend with the fact that the insertion of this song derails the tonal conflict that is arguably the medley's most important compositional strategy.

10. For a more detailed discussion of the incorporation of recording technique into the compositional process, see chapter 1.

11. Donald J. Grout and Claude V. Palisca, *A History of Western Music* (New York: W.W. Norton, 2006), 292.

12. Miles and McCartney, *Many Years from Now*, 306–7.

13. Miles and McCartney, *Many Years from Now*, 32–33.

14. Miles and McCartney, *Many Years from Now*, 70–71.

15. Henry W. Sullivan, *The Beatles with Lacan: Rock 'n' roll as Requiem for the Modern Age* (New York: P. Lang, 1995), 169.

7

MOVEMENT III:
"GOLDEN SLUMBERS"/
"CARRY THAT WEIGHT"/"THE END"

STEP ONE—HISTORICAL BACKGROUND

Recording, overdubbing, and mixing sessions for "Golden Slumbers"/ "Carry That Weight"/"The End" took place on July 24, 25, 29, and 30 and August 14 and 21, 1969.[1] Largely the work of lead vocalist Paul McCartney and producer George Martin, this track is often described, somewhat derisively, as the blueprint for McCartney's subsequent solo career. While there is some truth in this statement, it should also be noted that McCartney is the only ex-Beatle to continue to search for ways to expand the formal vocabulary of popular music beyond the limits of song form. Works such as "Uncle Albert"/"Admiral Halsey" (1971), "Hold Me Tight"/"Lazy Dynamite"/"Hands of Love"/"Power Cut" (1973), "Picasso's Last Words" (1973), and the album, *Back to the Egg* (1979) all bear testament to this view. His more recent experimentation with cyclic form in works such as *Liverpool Oratorio* (1994) and *Standing Stone* (1999) suggests a lingering fascination with this approach.[2]

STEP TWO—OPEN LISTENING

"Golden Slumbers" sounds remarkably like the opening section of Movement I. The tempo is restrained as before, but now the hopelessness that permeated "You Never Give Me Your Money" has given way to a sense of resolve. Perhaps this is due to the fact that the previous work was motivated by personal loss, whereas the focus here is on a collective sense of despair. It is also interesting to note that the lullaby promised in the verse and delivered in the chorus is not quiet and soothing but raucous and triumphant. This seems to underscore the narrator's sense of relief at being released from mournful isolation.

The celebration continues in "Carry That Weight," as a spirited male chorus asserts a collective determination to soldier on through life's trials and tribulations. In the middle of "Carry That Weight," the song that is the subject of this movement's re-composition ("You Never Give Me Your Money") is restated, first in instrumental form, then with vocals singing a modified text.

> I never give you my pillow
> I only send you my invitations
> And in the middle of the celebrations
> I break down.

The suggestion here is that the singer has modified his position and is no longer pointing the finger of blame at his partner. The resurfacing of melodic and lyrical material works well within the context of the re-composition that is being effected at deeper levels of the musical structure.

This remarkable moment is then followed by the return of "Carry That Weight" in an even more spirited manner than before. At its completion, the music presents yet another quote from Movement I, the 3+3+2 triadic figure that served as the underpinning for the nursery rhyme, "one, two, three, four, five, six, seven, all good children go to heaven." Suddenly, we are shifted by means of a remarkable edit into the transition that sets up the final section of Movement III. Riding on a climbing riff that recalls the octatonic bridge passage of Movement I, the lyric suggests that the entire medley has been a dream state from which we are about to awaken.

> Oh yeah, all right
> Are you going to be in my dreams
> Tonight?

As if to facilitate the awakening, drums enter playing a solo that is a miracle of primitive sophistication. Out of this spirited transition, there develops an elaborate three-way debate (McCartney, Harrison, Lennon) on electric guitar that derives its rhetorical power from the work's underlying harmonic strategy (double-tonic complex). As the guitars build to their inevitable climax, a solo piano enters with an insistent A major triad that sounds strangely out of tune. Here, the lead vocalist-narrator returns with a Shakespearean-styled couplet designed to wrap up the loose ends of the preceding nineteen minutes.

> And in the end the love you take
> Is equal to the love you make.

The work then ends on a climax of tonal and lyrical power that seems to resolve all of the paradoxes and contradictions that fascinated the Beatles throughout their career—and that ultimately served to drive them apart.

STEP THREE—MUSICAL SYNTAX

Key: A minor / C Major / A Major / C Major
Meter: 4/4
Form: Through-composed || A || B || C ||

Movement III seems a conscious recomposition of Movement I. As such, it is another through-composed form in which none of the major sections are repeated in any way. However, as in Movement II, each individual section is ingeniously structured so as to maintain a strong sense of forward motion. In particular, "Carry That Weight" features in its contrasting section, a full restatement of harmonic and melodic material that was first heard at the beginning of Movement I.

Since the various song fragments were recorded in two distinct sections, the following analysis will approach the movement in terms of this essential bipartite structure. As can be seen in the harmonic reduction (example 31), Movement III focuses mainly on a reexamination of the harmonic material first presented in Movement I.

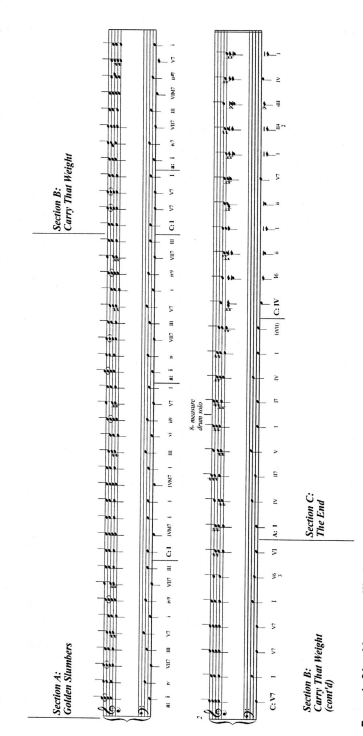

Example 31. Movement III—Harmonic Reduction

In addition to furthering the aforementioned double-tonic complex, this strategy helps infuse the medley with a strong sense of structural unity. Note how the stakes have been raised by the inclusion of the double tonic dialectic (A and C) within the body of each section. In "You Never Give Me Your Money" this relationship was expressed over the course of the entire movement, whereas here, it is integral to each section.

The genre-types in Movement III are fairly straightforward. All the models employed (rock ballad, anthem, blues-rock jam) seem well within the reach of a pop group of the late 1960s. There is, however, a subtle touch of integration at work in the chorus of "Golden Slumbers." Here, McCartney adopts a 1950s rock stance typical of performers such as Fats Domino and Jerry Lee Lewis. The piano plays a straight eighth-note pattern in the right hand while the left hand asserts the music's fundamental rhythmic accents.

Example 32.   Movement III—"Golden Slumbers"—(piano—chorus)

Note, however, that rather than using an F7 (F-A-C-Eb) in the second measure, McCartney employs an atypical Fmaj7 (F-A-C-E), thereby suggesting a blend of rock and jazz gestures. This lends the work a subtle poignancy not normally associated with traditional rock 'n' roll forms.

Part I—"Golden Slumbers"/"Carry That Weight"

As previously noted, Movement III re-composes harmonic material first presented in Movement I. The progression (i–iv–bVII–bIII) is identical in the first eight measures. At measure 8, the harmony moves briefly to the dominant of A minor before achieving a full cadence in the relative major at measure 11. Firmly placed for the moment in the key of C major, the chorus offers rhythmic contrast to the lyrical gestures of mm. 1–11. A disjunct melodic line is presented over a chord structure that, in its use of IVM7 in place of IV7, subtly modifies the traditional harmonic function typically associated with rock styles.

Example 33.   Movement III—"Golden Slumbers" (B Section)

There follows a full restatement of the opening section that is note-worthy for the countermelody presented in the cello line at mm. 23–24. At the conclusion of this verse (m. 30), "Carry That Weight" begins.

In its insistence on tonic and dominant harmony in the key of C ma-jor, "Carry That Weight" suggests an impending resolution to the A-C struggle. The anthemlike melodic line is predominantly stepwise, and thus well suited to the egalitarian tone of the text. At measure 39, the chorus of "Carry That Weight" begins with a full brass restatement of the opening measures of Movement I. This baroque-style gesture is then answered at measure 43 by an electric guitar, which varies the orig-inal material with blues-rock elements. At measure 46, the material pre-sented in instrumental form in mm. 39–45, is now performed in three-part vocal harmony with modified text. This is followed by a complete restatement of the verse between mm. 54–61, which is followed by the 3+3+2 pattern first heard during the final moments of Movement I.

Part II—"The End"

The first 10 measures of "The End" function as the first part of a tran-sition that tries once again to reassert the dominance of the tonal center of A over C. Measures 66 to 70 are presented in instrumental form while measures 71 to 76 feature vocals over the same harmonic and melodic structure. The rising progression in fourths also suggests a further con-nection with Movement I, in that it corresponds to the octatonic bridge

Example 34.   Movement III—"Golden Slumbers" (Cello Countermelody)

passage used to link "Out of College," "That Magic Feeling," and "One Sweet Dream."

Following the vocal line, the second part of the transition enters with an eight-measure drum solo that is remarkable for its spirited abandon within the confines of a highly organized tonal structure. At mm. 84–92, the full ensemble returns with vocals to lay the groundwork for the extended solos between mm. 93–111. This section features three electric guitars alternating in two-measure phrases over a repeating I7–IV7 progression in A Major.

Most remarkable is the fact that none of the lines in any of the individual solos employ a C#, the pitch that provides the defining quality to the A major chord.

Following the final guitar line (m. 110), a piano appears playing an insistent A major triad in eighth notes. The harmony is modified at measure 116 (G/A), suggesting that the implied root of the previous triad (A) was actually a pedal tone. This process is completed in measure 118 when an F major triad confirms that we are actually moving toward a resolution of the movement (and the medley) with a full cadence in C

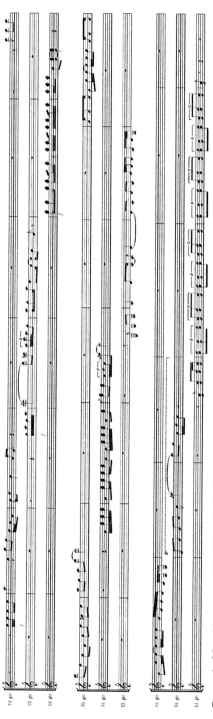

Example 35. Movement III—"The End" (Guitar Solos)

Example 36.   Movement III—"The End" (mm. 116–23)

major. This final example of mode mixture combines with a metric shift (duplets to triplets) to facilitate a smooth change in tempo for the movement's final measures.

A textural shift is also noted at measure 119 as the orchestra, last heard during "Golden Slumbers," returns to close the work. At measure 123, Movement III concludes following a plagal cadence in C major that decisively resolves the double-tonic complex first presented in Movement I.

Final Thoughts: Musical Syntax

The mode mixture first heard in Movements I and II is thoroughly integrated throughout Movement III. As such, it continues to act as the means of implementing the aforementioned double-tonic struggle. Throughout this movement, the two key areas (A and C) are continually set against one another with an intensity that builds toward the climactic guitar solos of "The End." When a solitary piano triad (A Major) emerges from the solos, it seems clear that the original tonal center has won out. Within several measures, however, A is destabilized to reveal the true winner: C.

Recording Strategies

As with "Sun King"/"Mean Mr. Mustard" and "Polythene Pam"/"She Came in Through the Bathroom Window," the third movement of the *Abbey Road* medley is an edit of two distinct takes. The basic tracks for "Golden Slumbers" and "Carry That Weight" were recorded on July 2, 1969, while "The End" was recorded on July 23, 1969. Otherwise, there are no exceptional recording strategies related to this movement. There is, however, a tuning anomaly that has yet to be explained to this writer's satisfaction.

At 4:37 into the track (m. 112), an acoustic piano reiterates an A major triad which is clearly not at concert pitch. From then on, the entire track is noticeably out of tune. Ian McDonald has suggested that this is the result of vari-speed techniques[3] being employed by EMI engineers during the extended guitar solos through mm. 93–111.[4] Although reasonable, this assertion seems unlikely, since guitar solos rarely require pitch alteration. A more likely culprit would be the three-part harmony vocals that appear in mm. 88–111. These are extremely high pitched, even for the Beatles. They also seem to be sung in full voice as opposed to light falsetto suggesting the involvement of women. Since no female vocalists are listed in any of the session notes for the medley, it seems more likely that it was the vocals and not the guitar solos that were recorded with the machine running slow so as to sound exceptionally high-pitched during playback.

STEP FOUR—THE SOUND-IN-TIME

A gently rocking piano line enters softly on the right channel. At 0:03, a vocalist enters in the center of the stereo spectrum and,, at 0:06, strings and electric bass appear, bathing the track in a smooth harmonic glow. At 0:33, drums announce the beginning of a new section that is decidedly more aggressive than the various sounds heard since the track first began. The singer belts assertively as drums, bass, piano, and strings provide rock-solid support from below. At 0:53, the drums withdraw to make way for the gentle return of the opening line. At 1:08, the strings become decidedly more active with an engaging line in the lower register. At 1:31, the drums once again enter to signal the beginning of a new section.

Now, a chorus of male voices joins the lead vocalist, and together they chant triumphantly as one. At 1:56, a majestic brass section enters with melodic material first heard during the opening of Movement I ("You Never Give Me Your Money"). At 2:07, the brass is answered by an electric guitar playing a blues-inflected variation. This is followed at 2:16 by a vocal restatement of the brass melody with a new text and, at 2:36, the full ensemble introduces a return of the chanted material first heard at 1:31.

At 3:08, an abrupt change is effected as electric guitars lead the ensemble in a rousing fanfare. At 3:19, this material is repeated with the addition of an impassioned lead vocal; at 3:27, guitars, bass, and vocals drop out to make way for a spiritedly lean drum solo. Relying heavily on the warm tones of the tom-toms and bass drum, this solo builds in intensity toward the explosive return of guitar and bass at 3:43. At 3:51, a vocal chorus in high tessitura joins the ensemble, paving the way for a three-way extended guitar solo that begins at 4:01.

At 4:37, all instruments drop out except for a solitary acoustic piano gently reiterating a triad in the middle of its register. At 4:41, the singer returns and is rapidly joined by the entire ensemble (including strings at 4:52). At 4:56, the music settles into a stately march as voices wordlessly trade lines with lead guitar. Following a majestic cadence at 5:05, the track fades into silence at 5:12.

STEP FIVE—MUSICAL AND TEXTUAL REPRESENTATION

Golden Slumbers

Once there was a way to get back homeward
Once there was a way to get back home
Sleep pretty darling do not cry
And I will sing a lullaby.

Golden slumbers fill your eyes
Smiles awake you when you rise
Sleep pretty darling do not cry
And I will sing a lullaby.

Once there was a way to get back homeward
Once there was a way to get back home
Sleep pretty darling do not cry
And I will sing a lullaby.

Carry That Weight

Boy, you're gonna carry that weight
Carry that weight a long time
Boy, you're gonna carry that weight
Carry that weight a long time.

I never give you my pillow
I only send you my invitation
And in the middle of the celebrations
I break down.

> Boy, you gonna carry that weight
> Carry that weight a long time
> Boy, you gonna carry that weight
> Carry that weight a long time.

The End

> Oh yeah, all right
> Are you going to be in my dreams tonight?
>
> And in the end the love you take
> Is equal to the love you make

On the surface level, the text of Movement III exhibits a return to the extended vowel sounds first heard in Section A from Movement I. Here, these vowels are employed within a syntactical structure that focuses on words associated with returns (way, homeward, home, sleep) thereby suggesting the end of a journey. On a deeper structural level, the text of Movement III offers a resolution to the conflicts at work in the previous two movements.

The opening number, "Golden Slumbers" is a curious adaptation of a lyric by the seventeenth-century English playwright Thomas Dekker.[5] McCartney makes adjustments to the model by using only the first stanza for the chorus of his own setting. It's interesting to note that the text here seems to answer the nursery rhyme/prayer that concluded Movement I:

> (Movement I)
> One two three four five six seven,
> All good children go to Heaven
> (Movement III)
> Sleep pretty darling do not cry
> And I will sing a lullaby.

In the coda of Movement I, the deep structure of the text projected fear and confusion as it prepared the listener for a journey that would lead beyond the temporal boundaries of conventional narrative structure. By contrast, the narrator of the text of "Golden Slumbers" assumes a

parental role in an apparent effort to soothe the fears and worries of a
now weary time-traveler (listener). Even though the chorus text and setting are more aggressively rendered, the message is still clear—things
will work out for the best.

In "Carry That Weight," the chorus sentiments of the previous track
are further explored in a message of encouragement that moves from lullaby to universal anthem as it attempts to give comfort to all of humanity.

> Boy, you're gonna carry that weight
> Carry that weight a long time

Following a brief restatement of the textual material from the opening
of Movement I now stripped of all solipsistic excess; the refrain of
"Carry That Weight" is repeated. This restatement lends the sentiment
even greater authenticity and power.

Significantly, "The End" opens and closes with what are essentially
two-line textual phrases. The first phrase seems to suggest that the preceding medley has taken place in a dream state that involved both performer and listener. The first couplet poses the question of whether this
relationship can once again be resumed in slumber.

> Oh yeah, all right
> Are you going to be in my dreams tonight?

Following a lengthy instrumental passage, the final couplet offers the
type of closure usually associated with Shakespearean drama.

> And in the end the love you take
> Is equal to the love you make.

Remarkably, this acknowledged pretension does not seem awkward or
forced.[6] In the concluding lyrical statement from their final recorded
work, the Beatles manage to be profound without trying.

STEP SIX—VIRTUAL FEELING

In its clever reworking of harmonic and lyrical material derived from
Movement I, the finale of the *Abbey Road* medley offers an appropri-

ate sense of return. The lullaby of "Golden Slumbers" functions simultaneously as soothing affirmation, and spirited call to arms. The call is then taken up in "Carry That Weight," as personal concerns become a very public matter. The reappearance of the mournful plea that opened Movement I resurfaces with a new optimism that seems the result of the previous song's words of encouragement. Following a restatement of "Carry That Weight," we move directly into the beginning of "The End."

The opening measures of "The End" are sustained by the words of encouragement first offered in "Golden Slumbers" and "Carry That Weight." Confidence abounds as the singer invites the listener to join him in subsequent dream states. At this point, lyrical content breaks off as a spirited drum solo propels the work forward toward its inevitable conclusion. An extended set of guitar solos that make up in wit and insouciance for what they lack in technical virtuosity responds to the challenge set forth by the drums. Theses solos create an intensity that seems fueled by the conflict at work within the medley's underlying tonal structure.

When it seems that the intensity can no longer be sustained, we break from full ensemble to a lonely acoustic piano, which in its reiteration of an A major triad, meekly claims victory in the ongoing harmonic struggle. The victory is short-lived however, since the music soon begins a measured slide down to the true winner of the contest: C major. Electric guitar and full orchestra solemnly lead the ensemble to a final cadence that promises stability for all concerned.

STEP SEVEN—ONTO-HISTORICAL WORLDS

The Beatles' importance to twentieth-century culture has yet to be fully realized. However, evidence suggests that the group's importance may lie in their remarkable ability to reconcile modernist and postmodernist aesthetic stances. As in Prelude "Because," which featured the instrumental pairing of an electric guitar with a baroque harpsichord, Movement III juxtaposes a baroque-style brass statement that is answered immediately by an electric guitar riddled with blue-note ornamentation. The stylistic dissonance created by using instruments of such widely disparate historical eras strengthens the argument that there is a modernist-postmodernist dialectic at work within the medley.

STEP EIGHT—OPEN LISTENINGS

As the medley moves toward its conclusion, one becomes conscious of a gradual rise in momentum, which is the result of various elements working together in a thoroughly integrated musical fabric. Of particular interest is the fact that the concluding section of Movement III ("The End") contains almost no lyrical content. Discounting the two-line phrases previously discussed, the bulk of this section is instrumental. This seems analogous to the final verse of Prelude "Because," in which wordless ululation took the place of structured text. Similarly in Movement III, it is the music itself that attempts to convey information that lies beyond the reach of discursive language.

STEP NINE—META-CRITIQUE

The greatest weakness of the preceding analysis was the fact that the analyst seemed overly involved in the drama of the work. As a result, the referential observations in steps five and six seemed especially heightened. It is possible that the nature of the data was simply reflecting structural developments in the work itself, but one should always attempt to maintain a critically reflective stance so as to offset the possibility of personal involvement having a negative impact on the analysis.

NOTES

1. Mark Lewisohn, *The Beatles' Recording Sessions* (New York: Harmony Books, 1988), 182–91.
2. Barry Miles and Paul McCartney, *Many Years from Now* (New York: H. Holt, 1997), 284.
3. A term used to describe analog recordings in which the speed of the tape machine is altered during the recording process. As a result, music

recorded in a particular key with the tape machine running slow would sound in a higher key during playback at normal speed. (See Lewisohn, *Recordings Sessions*, 204.)

4. Ian MacDonald, *Revolution in the Head: The Beatles' Records and the Sixties* (New York: H. Holt, 1994), 289.

5. Lewisohn, *Recordings Sessions*, 178.

6. Miles and McCartney, *Many Years from Now*, 558.

8

POSTLUDE—"HER MAJESTY"

STEP ONE—HISTORICAL BACKGROUND

Recorded on July 2, 1969, "Her Majesty" was one of the first sessions for the *Abbey Road* album following the June break, in which individual group members went on their respective holidays.[1] As previously noted, the song was originally slated for the midpoint between "Sun King"/ "Mean Mr. Mustard" and "Polythene Pam"/"She Came in Through the Bathroom Window." Its subsequent placement as the Postlude was arrived at through pure chance. At a listening session during which the song appeared serendipitously at the end of the master tape, the group members liked the effect so much that they decided to leave it in.[2] With this Cage-like flourish, the Beatles brought the medley, the album, and their entire career to a satisfying conclusion.

STEP TWO—OPEN LISTENING

The opening chord of "Her Majesty" wakes the listener out of complacency by its seeming incongruity. Following the majestic conclusion of Movement III, a full rock ensemble appears out of nowhere to play a spirited D-major triad and then departs. Out of the sound mass emerges a lone acoustic guitar accompanying a vocalist who sings a cheerful song of unrequited love. But the song is not about a fair maiden; instead, it is directed toward a member of the royal family. This is a love song to Queen Elizabeth!

The song itself is relatively straightforward but shows signs of the fusion of music hall and country-western styles. Its evident transposition from piano to acoustic guitar seems to have afforded Paul McCartney the opportunity to add some subtle brushstrokes to the work. The strumming is light but articulated, the singing assured yet understated. There is also an octave guitar slide during the bridge that lends a high degree of stylistic authenticity.

STEP THREE—MUSICAL SYNTAX

Key: D major
Meter: 2/2
Form: ‖ A ‖ A' ‖ B ‖ A" ‖

"Her Majesty" is an appropriate return to the refrain form that characterized Prelude "Because." Its construction is fairly regular, but this was probably deemed necessary in order to ground the rather eccentric character of the text. In effect, we are presented with a standard I–vi–II (V/V)–V–I progression that is typical of the song's folk, pop, and music-hall origins.

As can be seen in the following harmonic reduction (example 37), "Her Majesty" focuses on a tonal center (D major) that is closely re-

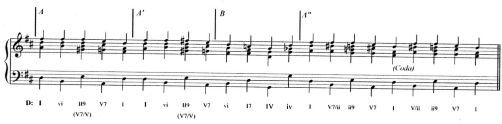

Example 37.   Postlude "Her Majesty"—Harmonic Reduction

lated (sub-dominant) to one of the key areas (A) that form a part of the medley's double-tonic structure. As such, it does not further the work's tonal strategy but instead seems to be a subtle postscript suggesting perhaps that although the tonal center of A came out second best in the medley-long struggle for dominance, there will be other contests on other days to come.

The key influence here seems to be George Formby, a popular twentieth-century British music-hall performer whose style was characterized by a lighthearted approach to serious subjects. Born in Liverpool, Formby was renowned for his high-pitched singing style and trademark ukulele accompaniment, which were featured in such songs as "When I'm Cleaning Windows" and "You Don't Need a License for That."[3] The influence of a ukulele style is particularly noticeable in the guitar voicing at measure 14 in which the composer-performer slides up an octave to play the root of a G minor triad on the D string.

Through the use of a descending bass line, "Her Majesty" offers harmonic variety within relatively narrow compositional parameters. The melody dances over the descending progression and features several nonharmonic tones that serve to extend the scope of the underlying harmonic structure.

Example 38.   Postlude "Her Majesty"—Verse (mm. 1–5)

Following a deceptive cadence (V–vi) at measure 10, there is a brief tonicization of the relative minor, which is consistent with the folk style of McCartney's compositional model. At measure 13, following a D7 chord that functions here as a secondary dominant, "Her Majesty" comes to a brief rest on IV.

At measure 14, the composer alters the IV chord heard in measure 13 by means of mode mixture. Now a minor subdominant, this chord initiates the final verse-coda, which consists of a I–VI (V/ii)–ii–V–I progression. Note the shift from the progression that formed the basis of mm. 1–10: the triad built on scale degree 2 (e) is now a minor chord. This change helps set up the final cadence on D, which is itself interrupted by an abrupt tape edit that leaves the music hanging unresolved on the fifth degree of the scale.

The thematic material of "Her Majesty" is predominantly conjunct in that it tends to outline elements of the underlying harmonic progression. However, there are several variations that tend to expand traditional diatonicism through the presence of jazz-derived musical gestures. In measure 4, the inclusion of an F# in the melody effectively transforms an E7 chord, functioning here as an applied dominant, into the more exotic E9.

Example 39.   Postlude "Her Majesty"—Verse (mm. 3–4)

This same technique is repeated again at measure 8. At measure 18, the same note (F#) is featured over an Em7 triad, thereby creating an Em9.

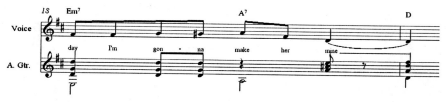

Example 40.   Postlude "Her Majesty"—Verse (m. 18)

Final Thoughts: Musical Syntax

The mode mixture first seen throughout the previous three move-ments is also briefly employed in "Her Majesty." But whereas it was pre-viously used to foreground the double-tonic complex that constitutes the medley's underlying tonal strategy, the use of a minor subdominant triad at m. 14 of "Her Majesty" is more likely a stylistic gesture charac-teristic of the compositional models upon which the work is based.

Recording Strategies

As previously noted, "Her Majesty" was recorded on July 2, 1969, as part of the first set of sessions that followed the group's month-long hol-iday in June. Since he lived relatively close to EMI Studios and gener-ally arrived at the sessions first, McCartney often took the opportunity to lay down demos of new material before the other members of the group arrived. In the case of "Her Majesty," the composer worked in a relatively simple fashion. Vocal and guitar are recorded on individual tracks for what is essentially a live performance.[4]

Following the opening triad (the final chord of "Mean Mr. Mustard" from Movement II) guitar and vocals enter in the center of the stereo spectrum. At 0:06, vocals and guitar pull to the right and remain there until 0:12 when they suddenly return to the center. One wonders whether this effect was achieved during the initial mixing sessions for the song or was perhaps seen as a necessary adjustment during attempts on July 30, 1969, to edit "Her Majesty" into the midpoint of Movement II.

During its initial entrance, "Her Majesty" exhibits some unusual au-ral effects. At 0:03, a sound—that presumably originates from McCart-ney's articulation on the fret board—echoes across the stereo spectrum as a high-pitched fluctuating squeak. It is unclear whether this sound is a result of reverb being used to create the impression that the music is emerging out of the distance or is perhaps an unintentional feedback between the two microphones used to record the vocals and the guitar accompaniment.

The cutoff on A natural (the fifth of the tonic triad) at the end of the track seems a further result of the aforementioned editing session on

July 30, 1969, in which the final cadence was deleted in order to make a clean transition into "Polythene Pam." As a result, the medley ends abruptly on a penultimate harmony.

STEP FOUR—THE SOUND-IN-TIME

After the seemingly interminable silence that followed the conclusion of Movement III, a full rock ensemble strikes and sustains a single chord. As suddenly as it emerged, the ensemble begins to fade away. At 0:02, an acoustic guitar and solo vocal emerge from the right channel. As the vocal/guitar performance continues, a series of high-pitched sounds are noticeable on the left channel. The guitar and vocalist can now be heard moving toward the center of the stereo spectrum. At 0:12, the music seems firmly centered. Gradually, however, one can perceive that it is still in motion, moving steadily toward the left channel. At 0:22, with guitar and vocal almost completely on the left channel, the piece concludes. Curiously, we never hear the final note. Instead, the sound cuts off sharply as if someone has accidentally cut the tape.

STEP FIVE—MUSICAL AND TEXTUAL REPRESENTATION

Her Majesty

> Her Majesty's a pretty nice girl,
> But she doesn't have a lot to say
>
> Her Majesty's a pretty nice girl
> But she changes from day to day.
>
> I want to tell her that I love her a lot
> But I gotta get a bellyful of wine
>
> Her Majesty's a pretty nice girl
> Someday I'm going to make her mine, oh yeah,
>
> Someday I'm going to make her mine.

On first reading, "Her Majesty" seems to be a simple genre parody. On the surface, the hard-edged vernacular conveys an unassuming man's absurd love for the sovereign. Gradually however, one is struck by an unexpected degree of poignancy that is increasingly evident on the level of deep structure. Although the narrator at first seems irreverent, it gradually becomes clear that he actually does love his queen. Her apparent reticence combined with the social distance between them helps create a touching portrait that moves effortlessly from personal affection to patriotic devotion.

STEP SIX—VIRTUAL FEELING

The opening chord comes as a shock following the soothing resolution of Movement III—but more surprises follow. Out of the sound mass caused by a full rock ensemble playing a single D-major triad, a lone acoustic guitar enters with a plaintive yet fervent declaration of love.[5] The light strumming style seems alternately carefree and solemn. The irreverent nature of the lyric is similarly undercut by a light vocal attack that suggests polite respect. As the work progresses, the combination of these elements reveals a level of poignancy not anticipated when the song first began. This quality is reinforced by the move to the relative minor, which coincides with the singer's declaration of unrequited love.

The final measures return to the irreverence of the opening lines as the singer declares his determination to make the queen his "girl." At the final cadence, we are suddenly left hanging on an unresolved fifth degree in the bass. The abruptness of this cutoff suggests that the tape has suffered an accidental edit but the jarring effect places "Her Majesty" in a new perspective. One wonders if someone has intentionally pulled the plug on the singer and that he has in fact been censored for disrespecting the monarch.

STEP SEVEN—ONTO-HISTORICAL WORLDS

In "Her Majesty," the wistfulness of the text is undercut by an essential irreverence that suggests a neoclassical parody of earnest love. McCartney has often approached form like a neoclassicist. In tracks like "Honey Pie" from *The Beatles* (1968), he borrows a 1920s dance-band template

that is authentic from the muted guitar fills, right down to the scratches
one would expect from an old 78rpm recording. As a result, he essentially delivers a "performance of a performance."[6] It is this very kind of
distancing that characterizes neoclassic art, that is, the desire by twentieth-century man to obscure his true feelings and never commit the sin
of being too obvious.[7] The narrator of "Her Majesty" exhibits this kind
of cagey reticence—but when the song ends, it's eminently clear that he
really does love his queen!

One should also take note of the additional distancing McCartney
achieves by placing feelings of patriotic devotion within the context of a
slight little ditty about unrequited love. Within the Beatles, he was reputedly the one who tended to resist any overt references to politics and
was reputedly alarmed by the increasingly militant stance taken by John
Lennon in the late 1960s.[8] He seemed to believe that part of the Beatles' essential strength lay in their remaining fundamentally apolitical.
One wonders then if "Her Majesty" could perhaps be viewed as an
anti–protest song in which the composer is attempting to obscure royal-
ist sentiment by couching it in an essential irreverence.

STEP EIGHT—OPEN LISTENINGS

The subtleties at work in "Her Majesty" were much more apparent during the second series of open listenings. In particular, the composer's attempts to veil establishment sentiments within what is essentially a
genre study were very impressive. Far from making the work seem dis-
honest or inauthentic, this narrative device contributes to the poignancy
achieved when the listener discovers that the singer is actually in
earnest. Another notable element is the virtuosity of the performance itself. The smooth tessitura of the vocals and the understated skill evident
in the guitar work were truly singular in their field—and bear testament
to the musicians' complete mastery of every level of their craft.

STEP NINE—META-CRITIQUE

The strengths of this analysis were particularly apparent in the sections
that focused on referential meaning, specifically, Musical and Textual

Representation, Virtual Feeling, and Onto-historical Worlds. Each of these levels revealed a remarkable sophistication at work within the song's narrative structure.

Additionally, the discussion of musical syntax afforded this writer an opportunity to consider the subtleties of the performance itself, which featured many nonchord tones in the vocal line, as well as an understated sophistication in the guitar accompaniment. The attempt to integrate recording strategies into the formal syntactical analysis seemed to be the most successful thus far. One could sense a flow in the discussion of multitrack technique and musical syntax, suggesting that further attempts at this kind of synthesis are warranted.

The historical analysis was less informative than in earlier sections. Since the work was already discussed in connection with its initial placement as the midpoint of Movement II, the data generated in the historical analysis seemed somewhat redundant. Additionally, the sound-in-time analysis of "Her Majesty" was less compelling than expected but this was probably due to the relative symmetry of the work as compared with earlier sections of the medley.

NOTES

1. Mark Lewisohn, *The Beatles' Recording Sessions* (New York: Harmony Books, 1988), 178.

2. Lewisohn, *Recording Sessions*, 183.

3. Colin Larkin, ed., *The Encyclopedia of Popular Music, Third Edition, Volume Three* (London: Muze UK, 1998), 1977–78.

4. Lewisohn, *Recording Sessions*, 178.

5. As previously noted, this is actually the final chord of "Mean Mr. Mustard" from Movement II. (See Lewisohn, *Recording Sessions*, 183)

6. On page 313 of the book *Tell Me Why* (New York: Knopf/Random House, 1988), Tim Riley uses a variation of this term ("performance-within-a-performance") to describe the conceptual approach taken by the Beatles on the album *Sgt. Pepper's Lonely Hearts Club Band* (1967).

7. Leonard Bernstein, *The Unanswered Question: Six Talks at Harvard* (Cambridge, MA: Harvard University Press, 1976), 375–79.

8. Ian MacDonald, *Revolution in the Head: The Beatles' Records and the Sixties* (New York: H. Holt, 1994), 237.

The Beatles in the Music Room

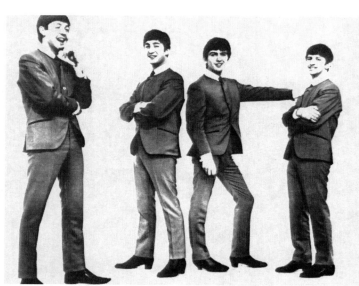

The Beatles
On February 7, 1964, the
Fab Four arrived in America
for the first time, to the
frenzied accompaniment
of thousands of screaming
teenagers. For the next six
years rock and roll spoke
with an English accent as
Beatlemania swept the
nation, inspiring a
generation of Americans to
form bands. *Shakespeares
in the Alley*, the third
episode in PBS's landmark
10-part series **Rock&Roll**,
airing Monday, September
25, 1995 at 9pm ET (check
local listings), chronicles the
Beatles' instant and ongoing
influence on rock and roll.
Photo: The Bettmann
Archive

The Beatles in 1963

Sir George Martin

The Beatles at Shea Stadium (August 1966)

The Beatles (circa 1965)

The Beatles in Milan (June 1965)

The Heady Days of Sgt. Pepper's Lonely Hearts Club Band *(1967)*

The Beatles' Final Photo Session at Tittenhurst Park (August 22, 1969)

Part III

CONCLUSIONS

9

AN IMPLICIT CHALLENGE

The purpose of this book has been to clarify the relationship between music recording and music composition through an analysis of a selected section of the album *Abbey Road* in order to characterize the emergent musical form. As demonstrated in the preceding eclectic analysis, this work employs a wide variety of progressive musical concepts firmly rooted in the Beatles' meticulous approach to multitrack recording. The data generated by the preceding chapters can now be collated and discussed with regard to the various levels of significance that formed the focus of this analysis.

FORMAL CONCLUSIONS

In its skillful articulation of an architectonic framework predicated on double-tonic relationships between the tonal centers of A and C, the *Abbey Road* medley displays a remarkable sophistication and musical eloquence. This framework facilitates the realization of a three-movement structure replete with sectional variation, thematic restatement, and inventive thematic and harmonic development. Building on the implicit challenge of works such as the Beach Boys' *Pet Sounds* (1966) and

Good Vibrations (1966) and the group's own *Sgt. Pepper's Lonely Hearts Club Band* (1967), the Beatles and their collaborators have succeeded in creating a viable extended form in the popular idiom.

Clearly, a musical achievement of this kind would not have been possible without the conscious integration of recording technology into the creative process. Such integration only became viable in the wake of the historical line of demarcation created by the premiere in 1958 of *Poeme Electronique*. As previously stated, this pivotal work by composer Edgard Varese delineated a shift in the functional definition of recording from archival documentation to what might be described as a reification of the "musical canvas." Consequently, the acoustical space associated with theaters and concert halls had now become a conceptual space, which the modern composer engages as the medium on which to "paint" musical sounds. As Virgil Moorefield writes:

> Originally, the aim of recordings was to create the illusion of a concert hall setting. The idea was to bring to the living room the sensation of being in a concert hall—a metaphor for presence. . . . There came into being a new conception of making records, developed separately and in stages, most notably by Phil Spector and George Martin. Although different in many ways, both of their approaches to production involved replacing the quest for the illusion of physical reality with a new aesthetic. The new sonic world they sought to create was the appearance of a reality which could not actually exist, a pseudo-reality created in synthetic space.[1]

The synthetic space Moorefield describes is analogous to the aforementioned reified musical canvas; it points to the Beatles' achievement in the *Abbey Road* medley as evidence of a complete mastery of the new sonic landscape made possible by the emerging technology of multitrack recording.

PHENOMENOLOGICAL CONCLUSIONS

The phenomenological approach affords the music analyst an opportunity to gain insight into the growth and development of the sound-in-time within an extended work. Freed from the exclusivity of formal methods of analysis, one is able to ponder the nature of form itself, not as a fixed template but rather as an ongoing process that a composer may partake of, though does not in fact initiate.

In *Philosophy and the Analysis of Music*, Ferrara asserts that "[f]or music listeners the word *music* has more of an active function than that of a simple noun and category. For these users of the term, *music* happens."[2] Correspondingly, in the essay "On the Value of Music and Music Education," David Elliott proposes a study of the significance of music as a diverse human practice. Essentially, he suggests that contemporary practitioners should define music not as a noun but rather as a verb.[3] Building on this idea, one could argue that the term *form*, as it currently exists in Western musical analysis, is too narrowly applied. In light of the phenomenological observations generated by this study of the *Abbey Road* medley, we might consider redefining *form* as a verb rather than a noun. In the course of a traditional musical analysis, one might therefore ask, How does this work form?

PHENOMENOLOGY OF RECORDING

In addition to allowing the analyst the opportunity to engage the music in a manner that avoids the presuppositions and assumptions that are a necessary characteristic of formal methods, phenomenology helps reveal the importance of recording techniques and their impact on the final composition. In a sense, the process of recording allows the modern composer/producer to orchestrate their music by employing elements more commonly associated with larger instrumental ensembles.

When writing for an orchestra, one is generally preoccupied with the importance of timbre and color—that is, the particular tonal qualities of musical instruments when played individually or in combination. The term *color* is apt since it points to the aspect of musical expression that lends itself to what might be described as the visualization of sound. In *Mix Masters: Platinum Engineers Reveal Their Secrets for Success*, engineer Geoff Emerick, a key collaborator on many late-period Beatles sessions (including *Abbey Road*), describes his approach to the recording process: "The way I approach it is I use what I'm given by the studio like a palette of paints. It's very hard to explain, but I hear visually. I hear certain sounds in different colors. It's really an art form to me. If you start asking me technical stuff, I'm not really that interested."[4] Emerick's comments emphasize the ways in which the advent of recording technique has afforded the artist the opportunity to actively incorporate timbre and color, ideas more commonly associated with traditional approaches to music composition.

REFERENTIAL CONCLUSIONS

Referential approaches to analysis can enable one to explore the possible meaning (or meanings) of a work based on cultural associations and historical consensus. The following discussion incorporates elements of musical and textual representation, virtual feeling, and onto-historical worlds with regard to their impact on the interpretative possibilities inherent in the *Abbey Road* medley.

So, What Might the Medley Mean?

Simply stated, the *Abbey Road* medley creates a narrative structure that attempts to process the paradigmatic shift from the modern to the postmodern era. In *The Beatles with Lacan*, Sullivan characterized the group as high priests symbolically presiding over a funeral for the Modern Era. He describes their role in Western culture as a celebration the old (modern) that was simultaneously involved in an active engagement of the new (postmodern).[5] The process Sullivan describes is evident in Prelude "Because," as musical and textual elements combine to create a dialectical relationship between modernist and postmodernist aesthetics. Here, the text and setting convey the singer's sense of wonder concerning the elemental properties of his life-world. The choice of a harpsichord as the primary instrument cleverly establishes an audible link with the baroque and pre-classical eras. The Beatles then double the harpsichord with electric guitar, an instrument that is predicated for its very existence on the development of modern technology. Through the skillful manipulation of its diverse musical and textual elements, Prelude "Because" conveys the experiences of an everyman living in late-twentieth-century Western culture. Poised as he was between two conflicting aesthetic paradigms (modern and postmodern), this everyman was rooted in a philosophical stance that put a premium on structural unity. At the same time, he was confronted by an emerging technology that increasingly portrayed the world in terms of a dazzling mosaic in which all attempts at thematic reduction seemed hopeless. As these two life-worlds collided, the everyman experienced a yearning for simplicity—a return to the garden. Prelude "Because" offers that return, but the garden it presents is a place where more questions are raised than are ultimately answered.

In an apparent attempt to adequately explore the philosophical questions posed by Prelude "Because," the narrative structure of Movement I—"You Never Give Me Your Money" focuses on the tenuous relationship between memory and present-day experience. By means of temporal references that are increasingly discontinuous as the work progresses, Movement I exhibits nuances that suggests a Proustian journey through what Susanne K. Langer has described as "experiential time."[6] Jarring temporal shifts are frequent throughout, as the isochronic narratives typical of popular music are subtly adapted toward the medley's larger purpose. Here, the everyman of Prelude "Because" begins to take stock of himself, and embarks on a journey through time in an effort to answer the aforementioned philosophical questions by assessing the data generated from personal experience.

By means of allegorical imagery and ingenious musical effects, Movement II offers a brief history of Western culture, circa 1700 to 1970. After experiencing the idealized landscapes of the "Sun King," we are confronted by a cultural environment that has been fundamentally altered by the pressures of an emerging industrialized society. Those who inhabit this new world (Mean Mr. Mustard and Polythene Pam) seem neurotic and solipsistic, perhaps as a result of the disillusionment engendered by the fragmentation of a dominant cultural paradigm. In "She Came in Through the Bathroom Window," the narrative lands in the present and continues to resonate with struggles engendered by the shift from modernism to postmodernism. The protagonists have inherited a world that is thoroughly perplexing in its paradoxes and contradictions. The storyline presumably concerns a young man and woman of marrying age who are attempting to find their way through an abstract associational landscape. Despite the evident confusion, they are ultimately able to survive by focusing on the one human element common to all eras—love.

In its clever reworking of harmonic and lyrical material, the finale of the *Abbey Road* medley offers an appropriate sense of return. The lullaby that is "Golden Slumbers" functions simultaneously as a soothing affirmation and a spirited call to arms. This call is taken up in "Carry That Weight," through a text in which personal concerns are correlated with public responsibility. The opening measures of "The End" are sustained by the words of encouragement first offered in "Golden Slumbers"/ "Carry That Weight." Confidence abounds as the singer invites the listener to join him in subsequent dream states. At this point, lyrical content breaks off as a rousing drum solo propels the work forward toward its inevitable conclusion. The extended guitar solos that follow build in an angry intensity that seems fueled by the tonal conflict at work within the medley's double-tonic structure. When it seems that this tension can no longer be sustained, we suddenly break from the full ensemble to a lonely acoustic piano that meekly claims victory in the lingering harmonic struggle by insistently reiterating an A major triad. This apparent victory is short-lived, however, as the ensemble subsequently begins a measured slide down to the true winner of the tonal struggle: C major. Electric guitar and full orchestra solemnly lead the ensemble to a final cadence that promises stability for all concerned.

It should also be noted that as in Prelude "Because," which featured the pairing of electric guitar with harpsichord, Movement III presents a baroque-style brass statement that is immediately answered by an electric guitar line riddled with blue-note ornamentation. The stylistic dissonance created by using instruments and styles of such widely disparate historical eras lends weight to the argument that there is a fusion of modernist and postmodernist aesthetics at work within the *Abbey Road* medley.

Following the soothing resolution offered at the conclusion of Movement III, the opening chord of the Postlude, "Her Majesty," comes as something of a shock. Out of the sound mass created by a full rock ensemble playing a single D-major triad, a lone acoustic guitar enters with a plaintive, yet fervent declaration of love.[7] The strumming style seems alternately carefree and solemn and the irreverent nature of the lyric is similarly undercut by a light vocal attack that suggests polite respect. As the work progresses, this combination reveals a level of poignancy not anticipated when the song first began. The final measures return to the irreverence of the opening lines as the singer declares his determination to make the queen his girl. At the closing cadence, we are suddenly left hanging on an unresolved fifth degree in the bass. This remarkable effect draws attention to the integration of recording technology into the compositional process and creates the impression that the *Abbey Road* medley has ended "in progress."[8]

FUTURE DEVELOPMENT

In the *Abbey Road* medley, the band has arguably presented a viable solution to the dilemma brought on by the end of the modern era. By leaning on traditional methods of musical construction, while simultaneously embracing recording technology as part of the compositional process, it has offered Western culture a way out. In this work, Wagnerian and Beethovenian double-tonic structures exist side by side with nine-part vocal overdubs, while classical mode mixture is presented interchangeably with the creative flexibility afforded by elaborate tape edits. The medley thus posits a viable synthesis between the modern and the postmodern, two seemingly antithetical aesthetic stances. Whether we can respond to the cultural challenge implicit in the Beatles' final recorded work remains to be seen. As author Henry W. Sullivan writes:

> In all aspects of their creative activity and influence, they sent the message to their fans that another kind of logic, or way of knowing, was to be sought and, perhaps, encountered. Inasmuch as these insights still remain to be articulated in a more communicable form, we have not as yet returned the Beatles a satisfactory answer to their message.[9]

Subsequent Influence

Although we may not as yet have given the Beatles a satisfactory answer to the challenges posed by their final recorded work, many talented composer-performers have certainly tried. In an effort to demonstrate the influence of the *Abbey Road* medley on popular composers of the 1970s, the following works will now be briefly discussed with regard to the development of extended forms in popular musical practice.

"Uncle Albert"/"Admiral Halsey" (Paul McCartney, 1971)

As previously stated, Paul McCartney is the only former Beatle who has continued to explore the possibilities of extended form in his solo career. His album *Ram* (1971) appears to be patterned on *Sgt. Pepper's Lonely Hearts Club Band* (1967) in its overall design and, as such, does little to directly advance the notion of extended form. However, it does constitute an attempt to create another work in the same idiom and thereby bears out *Pepper's* claim for the validity of concept albums (and/or song cycles) in popular music.[10] With its lyrical free association and subtle changes in texture and style, track 5—"Uncle Albert"/ "Admiral Halsey" does suggest the further development of an *Abbey Road* aesthetic. However, despite its melodic and structural ingenuity, this track does not exhibit the organic unity necessary to qualify it as an individual movement.

Dark Side of the Moon (Pink Floyd, 1973)

Following the departure of founding member Syd Barrett in 1968, the British rock band Pink Floyd began to move steadily toward the conceptual approach that is now commonly regarded as the hallmark of the group's best work.[11] Interestingly, the songs achieve movementlike status by means of slow tempos and stark instrumental textures. The band's landmark album *Dark Side of the Moon* (1973) is still highly regarded for its musical acumen as well as its progressive approach to recording technology. Since it is best appreciated on CD where one can hear the songs consecutively without interruption, it may well represent Floyd's most successful attempt to surpass the *Abbey Road* medley, by creating a large form that extends beyond one side of a vinyl LP.

"Scenes from an Italian Restaurant" (Billy Joel, 1977)

As one of the most successful songwriters of the post-Beatles era, Billy Joel has always been forthright in acknowledging the group's considerable influence on his own compositional style. Following a series of journeyman albums released in the early 1970s, he recorded *The Stranger* (1977) in collaboration with producer Phil Ramone. The album's centerpiece, "Scenes from an Italian Restaurant," employs a remarkable multipart structure that suggests the internal processes of a one-movement sonata. Reminiscent of "You Never Give Me Your Money," "Scenes" is arguably one of the most fully realized works based on the *Abbey Road* medley to date.[12]

RECOMMENDATIONS FOR FURTHER STUDY

This book has endeavored to clarify the relationships between music recording and music composition through an analysis of the *Abbey Road* medley. The adaptation of Ferrara's eclectic method to incorporate detailed discussions of recording techniques in order to ascertain their possible impact on the process of music composition suggests a possible advance in methodological practice. It seems reasonable to assert that future research into the analysis of popular music could benefit from the techniques employed in this study.

Although the data generated by this analysis have arguably contributed to a deeper understanding of a complex aesthetic process, it is clear that much more research is needed. In a sense, the *Abbey Road* medley is only the tip of the iceberg. Since contemporary musicians increasingly experience music composition as a practice that exists in tandem with the continually evolving art of sound recording, the greatest obstacle to further research is the general unavailability of the multitrack masters that constitute the true score of a recorded work.

The frustration that results from the inability to examine master tapes is palpable in many Beatles studies. For example, Walter Everett's essay "The Beatles as Composers: The Genesis of *Abbey Road*, Side Two" builds on the research of historian Mark Lewisohn and presents track breakdown diagrams in an effort to illuminate the distinctive nature of the recording process as it relates to the final creation of a musical work.[13] Despite the ingenuity of these diagrams, one quickly realizes that this intriguing aspect of Everett's research is essentially incomplete due to his inability to access the original multitrack masters.

Like the work of Everett, this study has relied heavily on Mark Lewisohn's texts on the Beatles' activities at EMI Studios in the 1960s. In the early 1980s, Lewisohn was granted unprecedented access to the studio archives and, as a result, was able to provide an authoritative account of the Beatles' approach to multitrack recording. His book *The Beatles Recording Sessions* (1988) features detailed session note transcriptions, as well as comments by band members, session players, and relevant studio personnel.[14] Mr. Lewisohn's work is certainly meticulous and very enlightening but it can only take one so far. It is therefore necessary for the researcher to continue to try to get as close to the source material as possible.

Fortunately, the reissue of the Beatles' 1995 documentary, *Anthology*, on DVD contains an additional eighty-one minutes (approximately) of documentary material which includes footage of the surviving Beatles and producer George Martin at EMI Studios in May 1995 examining the master reels of several groundbreaking Beatles tracks. One of the tracks they examined was "Golden Slumbers," the song that constitutes the opening section of Movement III of the *Abbey Road* medley. Here, McCartney, Harrison, Starr, and Martin comment on the sessions for the *Abbey Road* album and also share many insights concerning the nature and origin of the experimentation prevalent at EMI studios during the 1960s.[15]

Although the insights featured in this documentary footage were an invaluable aid in the completion of this book, a detailed examination of the original master tapes would have greatly enhanced all aspects of the analysis. At this point however, EMI still retains complete ownership of the Beatles' recordings, and only a select few have been granted the opportunity to carefully examine this archival material. Understandably, the dangers of tape degeneration resulting from repeated playbacks would seem to work against the possibility of open access to the master tapes. Technology, however, may soon provide a solution to this problem.

In 1994, popular musician and composer Todd Rundgren released *No World Order*, an album that actively engaged the intriguing possibilities engendered by the emerging computer-based technology. In an article for the online journal *Digital Culture*, Scott Rosenberg described this work's revolutionary approach to musical creation:

> Todd Rundgren's approach . . . is to focus almost exclusively on music alone. You set some controls on *No World Order*, specifying your preferences in mood, tempo, mix, and so forth. Then the disk plunders its database of musical bits and pieces and assembles a version of itself to your

specifications; change your orders, and the music changes too; . . . the core of the art itself, the music, alters based on your input; . . . and the results feel less like a musical interaction between you and Rundgren than a kind of musical equivalent to William Burroughs's cut-up technique of chopping and reassembling texts.[16]

Considering the interactive nature of Rundgren's release, it seems feasible that albums such as *Abbey Road* could be made available in multitrack format on DVD-ROM. The serious researcher (or casual listener) would thus have the opportunity to closely examine the individual tracks, early takes, and alternate mixes that ultimately led to the realization of the finished work. Such a development would greatly enhance our understanding of the evolving relationship that exists between music recording and music composition.

In the meantime, since further research is needed to situate sound recording within the realm of compositional praxis, this writer will continue to incorporate discussions of recording technique into the analysis of musical syntax. Future musicologists are wholeheartedly encouraged to do the same.

NOTES

1. Virgil Edwin Moorefield, "From the Illusion of Reality to the Reality of Illusion: The Changing Role of the Producer in the Pop Recording Studio," Ph.D. diss. (Princeton, NJ: Princeton University, 2001), viii.

2. Lawrence Ferrara, *Philosophy and the Analysis of Music* (New York: Greenwood Press, 1991), xiii. Indeed, in Ferrara's discussion of Heidegger's philosophy, he notes that in Heidegger's engagement of the fundamental question of ontology, Being, he transforms the very notion of Being from noun to verb (104).

3. David Elliott, "On the Value of Music and Music Education," *Philosophy of Music Education Review* 1, no. 2 (Fall 1993): 81–92. This proposal was further developed in Elliott's book, *Music Matters: A New Philosophy of Music Education* (1995).

4. Maureen Droney, *Mix Masters: Platinum Engineers Reveal Their Secrets for Success* (Boston: Berklee Press; Milwaukee: distributed by Hal Leonard, 2003), 183.

5. Henry W. Sullivan, *The Beatles with Lacan: Rock 'n' Roll as Requiem for the Modern Age* (New York: P. Lang, 1995), 153–70.

6. Susanne K. Langer, *Feeling and Form: A Theory of Art* (New York: Scribner, 1953), 109.

7. As previously noted, this is actually the final chord of "Mean Mr. Mustard" from Movement II. (See Lewisohn, *Recording Sessions*, 183.)

8. Terence J. O'Grady, *The Beatles: A Musical Evolution* (Boston: Twayne Publishers, 1983), 164. O'Grady uses this term in reference to the entire *Abbey Road* album. It is used here solely in reference to the *Abbey Road* medley.

9. Sullivan, *The Beatles with Lacan*, 169.

10. On the *Ram* album, McCartney's approach to timbre, within the context of arrangement and production, suggests the influence of the Beach Boys' *Pet Sounds* (1966).

11. Stanley Sadie, ed., *The New Grove Dictionary of Music and Musicians, Second Edition, Volume Nineteen* (New York: Thames & Hudson, 2001), 755–56.

12. Sadie, ed., *New Grove Dictionary, Volume Thirteen*, 134–35.

13. Walter Everett, "The Beatles as Composers: The Genesis of *Abbey Road*, Side Two," in *Concert Music, Rock, and Jazz since 1945: Essays and Analytical Studies*, ed. Elizabeth West Marvin and Richard Hermann (Rochester, NY: University of Rochester Press, 1995), 172–228.

14. In 2006, Kevin Ryan and Brian Kehew completed their self-published work, *Recording the Beatles: The Studio Equipment and Techniques Used to Create Their Classic Albums* (Houston: Curvebender Publishers, 2006). Their book effectively expands on Mark Lewisohn's seminal research by creating an in-depth analysis of recording practices at the Abbey Road Studios during the 1960s. Within the context of their discussion, the authors employ track diagrams similar to the ones used by Walter Everett.

15. *The Beatles Anthology*, DVD, directed by Geoff Wonfor (London: Apple Corps Limited, 2003).

16. Scott Rosenberg, "Peter Gabriel and Todd Rundgren Attempt to Interact with You," *Digital Culture*, 1994, http://www.wordyard.com/dmz/digicult/cdmusic-5-1-94.html (July 15, 2007).

APPENDIX A:
REVIEW OF RELATED LITERATURE

Since they first appeared on the British music charts in 1962, there's been a steadily growing body of research on the music of the Beatles. For the most part, this research has tended to examine the group from a fan-based cultural or philosophical perspective. Recent studies, however, have moved away from explanations of what the group represents and focused instead on a more detailed analysis of what the Beatles actually did. This shift in the focus of Beatles scholarship can be characterized in terms of a gradual foregrounding of the group's creative process.

In December of 1963, *The London Times* printed an article on the music of the Beatles by their leading music critic, William Mann. His review was widely cited for its comparison of Beatles songs with the music of Gustav Mahler:

> [T]he slow, sad song about "This Boy," which features prominently in Beatle programmes, is expressively unusual for lugubrious music, but harmonically it is one of their most intriguing, with its chains of pandiatonic clusters, and the sentiment is acceptable because voiced cleanly and crisply. But harmonic interest is typical of their quicker songs, too, and one gets the impression that they think simultaneously of harmony and melody, so firmly are the major tonic sevenths and ninths built into their tunes, and the flat—submediant key—switches, so natural is the Aeolian

cadence at the end of "Not a Second Time" (the chord progression which ends Mahler's *Song of the Earth*).[1]

Mann's approach is typical of early critiques of the Beatles' work in that it attempts to reconcile the more progressive elements in the group's music with established masterworks of the Western musical canon. Although helpful with regard to syntactical and stylistic relevance, Mann's review does little to illuminate the unique quality of the Beatles' approach to compositional method.

In 1968, Hunter Davies's *The Beatles: The Authorized Biography* offered another perspective. Since the group had contracted the author to produce the book under their careful supervision, there is little to be found in the nature of in-depth analysis. However, Davies was granted access to the Beatles' inner circle and, as a result, attended several pivotal writing and recording sessions. During the recording of *Sgt. Pepper's Lonely Hearts Club Band* (1967), he was allowed to observe the group layering vocal parts onto the track "Getting Better" and commented on the seemingly tedious nature of the process.[2] More significant was his presence at a Lennon-McCartney writing session at Paul McCartney's home in St. John's Wood, London, during which both composers brainstormed ideas for the *Sgt. Pepper's* track "With a Little Help from My Friends."[3]

The next serious research came in 1973 with the publication of Wilfred Mellers's *Twilight of the Gods: The Music of the Beatles*. A respected academic, Mellers used formal analytical methods in an attempt to ground referential elements concerning the mythopoeic nature of the Beatles phenomenon. Most interesting was his assertion that *Sgt. Pepper's Lonely Hearts Club Band* constituted "the most distinctive event in pop's brief history"[4] since it was the point at which rock 'n' roll became music to be listened to rather than a background for ritualistic dance.[5] Although his text offered some of the most detailed transcriptions produced to that point, Mellers's speculations on the cultural relevance of the group's complex iconography tended to move the discussion away from the notion of process.

Throughout the late 1970s, publications on the Beatles tended to focus on biographical accounts of the group's real or imagined history. As a result, few new insights were offered. An exception, however, was

George Martin's *All You Need Is Ears* (1979) in which the Beatles' record producer provided detailed descriptions of the group's creative process in the recording studio, as well as informed assessments of the respective compositional styles of John Lennon, Paul McCartney, and George Harrison.[6]

In 1983, Terence J. O'Grady's *The Beatles: A Musical Evolution* presented the first attempt by a member of the academic community to provide a purely musical analysis of the Beatles' entire recorded output. He structured his work on a three-period model that attempted to describe the group's remarkable stylistic development between 1963 and 1970. O'Grady's text is noteworthy for its meticulous scholarship and its clear potential as a pedagogical text.[7] The year 1983 also saw the publication of Peter Brown's *The Love You Make: An Insider's Story of the Beatles*. Following the death of manager Brian Epstein in 1967, Mr. Brown, formerly Epstein's personal assistant, acted as the group's de facto manager until their ultimate dissolution in 1970. As such, his insights are an invaluable source for qualitative research. Like Martin's *All You Need Is Ears*, Brown's book is an authoritative account of the Beatles' creative dynamic by someone who witnessed the events firsthand.[8]

In 1988, Tim Riley's *Tell Me Why* provided a detailed commentary on the entire Beatles' catalog. Riley's text exhibits a wide-ranging understanding of Beatles and solo Beatle recordings but rarely provides any syntactical evidence on which to ground his own critical observations about their music. This is particularly confusing since the book's liner notes describe him as a trained pianist and, therefore, exceptionally well qualified to give authoritative assessments of the Beatles' musical worth. However, the book is well written, and its ambitious scope makes it a useful resource for popular music research.[9]

Arguably, the most important development in Beatles research came in late 1988 with the publication of Mark Lewisohn's *The Beatles' Recording Sessions*. In the mid-1980s, Lewisohn was granted unprecedented access to the EMI studio archives and as a result was able to provide an authoritative account of the Beatles' approach to sound recording. His book features detailed session note transcriptions, as well as interviews with session players and relevant studio personnel. Subsequent Beatles scholars would rely heavily on the Lewisohn text as primary source material and as a model for quantitative and qualitative research.[10]

In 1993, Wise Publications issued *The Beatles: Complete Scores*, a book that provided detailed transcriptions for all of the group's official releases. Each song is presented in full score—that is, with drums, guitar, bass, piano, and vocals. Regrettably however, no detailed orchestral transcriptions were included. Whenever necessary, the authors simply provide an additional staff and an appropriate triad with the designation *brass, strings,* or *woodwinds.* In spite of this shortcoming, this ambitious work must be acknowledged as a major step forward in the field of Beatles scholarship.[11]

Armed with fresh insight into the group's creative process as a result of the Lewisohn text and *The Beatles: Complete Scores*, recent works have attempted to understand the group within a larger sociological or cultural context. In this regard, Ian MacDonald's *Revolution in the Head* (1994) is particularly significant. In a fascinating introductory essay, MacDonald attempts to explain, from a philosophical perspective, what the Beatles' music actually means. His book is well researched and relies heavily on the Lewisohn text for information concerning the recording process.[12] Mark Hertsgaard's *A Day in the Life: The Music and Artistry of the Beatles* (1995) is also interesting in its attempts to reconcile the Beatles' achievements with a late-twentieth-century cultural perspective.[13] On May 1, 1995, a review of both the MacDonald and Hertsgaard texts appropriately titled "Carry That Weight" appeared in the *New Yorker* magazine. In that review, critic Adam Gopnik made a fascinating observation on the Beatles' approach to songwriting: "What made them special was not conviction but a new kind of humor—ironic distance without disdain. Everything seems to happen in the comic conditional: If I were actually in love with a girl, this is the kind of song I would sing."[14] Gopnik's comments go to process and intent and thus generate pertinent questions with regard to the analysis of both form and reference.

In 1995, Henry W. Sullivan published *The Beatles with Lacan: Rock 'n' Roll as Requiem for the Modern Age.* By utilizing the psychological theories of Jacques Lacan, the author attempted to explain the Beatles' creative dynamic from the standpoint of subconscious motivation and personal trauma. He focused primarily on the relationship between John Lennon and Paul McCartney, which he claimed was the essence of the group's distinctive collective identity. Sullivan also framed his premise on the notion that the Beatles played a pivotal role in Western culture's transition into postmodernism. As such, their work is able to resonate on various levels in the collective unconscious and is particularly well suited as an elegy for the modern era.[15]

Since the mid 1990s, a series of doctoral dissertations have appeared that attempt to deal with the music of the Beatles as it relates to the development of the recording process. One is particularly relevant to this book. In "From the Illusion of Reality to the Reality of Illusion: The Changing Role of the Producer in the Pop Recording Studio (2001)," Virgil Edwin Moorefield deals with the effects of recording technology on the composition of popular music. Moorefield's study seeks to foreground the expanded role of the producer in the wake of the development of a new musical aesthetic engendered by the advent of multitrack recording.[16]

Also deserving of mention is the work of music theorist Alan Pollock. In the early 1990s, Pollock began publishing an online text, which presented brief yet remarkably thorough analyses of Beatle songs. Although somewhat lacking in detailed syntactical description, Pollock's work does attempt to incorporate an awareness of recording technique into the body of his analyses. In connection, the website that features Pollock's work, Soundscapes.info, offers a variety of articles and essays focusing on the scholarly analysis of popular music.[17]

Walter Everett's recent two-volume work, *The Beatles as Musicians: Revolver through* The Anthology (1999) and *The Beatles as Musicians: The Quarry Men through* Rubber Soul (2001) represents the culmination of an ongoing effort to illuminate the Beatles' unique approach to the musical process.[18] Building on the strengths of previous studies by Wilfred Mellers, Terence O'Grady, and Mark Lewisohn, Everett's text exhibits a thoroughly informed understanding of the Beatles' entire catalog. Principally, his work represents an increasing willingness on the part of the academic community to develop an integrated understanding of the Beatles' music.[19]

In 2002, Ian Peel published *The Unknown Paul McCartney: McCartney and the Avant-Garde*. This fascinating study focuses on Paul McCartney's experimental work in the late Beatles period and beyond. Peel describes the considerable influence of composers such as John Cage, Karlheinz Stockhausen, and Steve Reich on the music of the Beatles and also documents how, in his solo career, McCartney continually attempted to create works that challenged conventional notions about what was possible in popular music.[20]

In 2003, author Maureen Droney published *Mix Masters: Platinum Engineers Reveal Their Secrets for Success*, a collection of interviews with twenty-seven influential studio engineers who had a significant impact on the development of recorded sound in the late twentieth century. Of particular interest was an in-depth interview with Geoff Emerick, the engineer who had worked closely with the Beatles between 1966 and 1969. During the course of this interview, Emerick discussed the various recording innovations he had conceived and/or implemented at EMI Studios at the behest of the Beatles and producer George Martin.[21] His insights are an invaluable resource with regard to the incorporation of recording strategies into the analysis of musical syntax.[22]

In 2003, Apple Records rereleased the Beatles' 1995 documentary *The Beatles' Anthology* on DVD. Significantly, this rerelease contained an additional eighty-one minutes (approximately) of documentary material, in which the surviving Beatles and producer George Martin meet at Abbey Road Studios to deconstruct the masters of several groundbreaking Beatles tracks. Included among these was "Golden Slumbers," the song that constitutes the opening section of Movement III of the *Abbey Road* medley. The group members comment on the sessions for the album and share their insights concerning the nature of the experimentation prevalent at Abbey Road during the 1960s.[23]

Finally, on August 5, 2003, this writer conducted an interview with Peter Brown, author of *The Love You Make: An Insider's Story of the Beatles*. As previously stated, Brown was personal assistant to Brian Epstein in the early part of the Beatles' career and following Epstein's death became the group's de facto manager. As a result, he was directly involved in the day-to-day operations at Apple Corps from 1968 through 1970. During the course of the interview, Brown offered numerous insights into the Beatles' distinctive creative dynamic and also provided fascinating background information on the cultural context from which the group emerged.[24]

NOTES

1. William Mann, "What Songs the Beatles Sang . . . ," *The Times* (Dec. 27, 1963): 4, quoted in David Brackett, ed., *The Pop, Rock, and Soul Reader: Histories and Debates* (New York: Oxford University Press, 2005), 172–73.

2. Hunter Davies, *The Beatles* (New York: W.W. Norton, 1978), 26, 871.

3. Hunter Davies, *The Beatles*, 263–68.

4. *The Compleat Beatles*, VHS, directed by Patrick Montgomery (New York: MGM/UA Home Video 1982), comments transcribed by author.

5. Wilfrid Mellers, *The Twilight of the Gods: the Music of the Beatles* (New York: Viking Press, 1973), 86.

6. George Martin and Jeremy Hornsby, *All You Need Is Ears* (New York: St. Martin's Press, 1979).

7. Terence J. O'Grady, *The Beatles: A Musical Evolution* (Boston: Twayne Publishers, 1983).

8. Peter Brown, *The Love You Make: An Insider's Story of the Beatles* (New York: McGraw-Hill, 1983).

9. Tim Riley, *Tell Me Why: A Beatles Commentary* (New York: Knopf/Random House, 1988).

10. Mark Lewisohn, *The Beatles' Recording Sessions* (New York: Harmony Books, 1988). In 2006, Kevin Ryan and Brian Kehew expanded on Lewisohn's research with their book *Recording the Beatles: The Studio Equipment and Techniques Used to Create Their Classic Albums*. This self-published work, available only through the authors' website, presents an in-depth analysis of recording practices at Abbey Road during the 1960s. It also provides an overview of the Beatles' studio work and a discussion of the techniques used to create a wide variety of individual tracks. As such, it serves as an invaluable resource for those wishing to explore the connections that exist between music composition and sound recording.

11. Beatles, *The Beatles: Complete Scores* (London, New York, and Milwaukee, WI: Wise Publications, 1993).

12. Ian MacDonald, *Revolution in the Head: The Beatles' Records and the Sixties* (New York: H. Holt, 1994).

13. Mark Hertsgaard, *A Day in the Life: The Music and Artistry of the Beatles* (New York: Delacorte Press, 1995).

14. Adam Gopnik, "Carry That Weight." Review of Hertsgaard's *A Day in the Life* and MacDonald's *Revolution in the Head* in *The New Yorker* (May 1, 1995).

15. Henry W. Sullivan, *The Beatles with Lacan: Rock 'n' roll as Requiem for the Modern Age* (New York: P. Lang, 1995).

16. Virgil Edwin Moorefield, "From the Illusion of Reality to the Reality of Illusion: The Changing Role of the Producer in the Pop Recording Studio," Ph.D. diss. (Princeton, NJ: Princeton University, 2001). Moorefield has since adapted his dissertation into a fascinating book, *The Producer as Composer: Shaping the Sounds of Popular Music* (Cambridge, MA: MIT Press, 2005).

17. Alan W. Pollock, "Alan W. Pollock's Notes on . . . Series," Soundscapes .Info, 1999, http://www.icce.rug.nl/~soundscapes/DATABASES/AWP/awp-notes _on.shtml (July 15, 2007).

18. Walter Everett, *The Beatles as Musicians: Revolver Through the* Anthology (New York: Oxford University Press, 1999).

19. Walter Everett, *The Beatles as Musicians: The Quarry Men through* Rubber Soul (New York: Oxford University Press, 2001).

20. Ian Peel, *The Unknown Paul McCartney: McCartney and the Avant-Garde* (London and Richmond, Surrey: Reynolds & Hearn, 2002.).

21. Maureen Droney, *Mix Masters: Platinum Engineers Reveal Their Secrets for Success* (Boston: Berklee Press; Milwaukee: distributed by Hal Leonard, 2003).

22. During the research that went into the preparation of this book, I attempted to secure an interview with Mr. Emerick. Unfortunately, at that time he was busy preparing a book on his own experience of working with the Beatles, which has since been published. Emerick's *Here, There, and Everywhere* is a fascinating account of the development of the group's recording praxis and is essential reading for all those wishing to gain a deeper appreciation of the Beatles' musical and cultural significance: Geoff Emerick, *Here, There, and Everywhere: My Life Recording the Music of the Beatles* (New York: Gotham Books, 2006).

23. *The Beatles Anthology*, DVD, directed by Geoff Wonfor (London: Apple Corps Limited, 2003).

24. Peter Brown, in discussion with the author, Aug. 5, 2003.

APPENDIX B:
INTERVIEW WITH PETER BROWN

August 5, 2003

THOM: So, how aware were the members of the group, particularly John Lennon and Paul McCartney, of their importance in musical history?

PETER: At this point?

THOM: By 1968, there are interviews with McCartney where he states that they (the Beatles) were very aware of the importance of what they did with regard to musical development. Was this something that you were cognizant of?

PETER: Yes, I mean you could not, *not* be aware because of the success. And, you know, their success was so unique in the fact that non-American musicians-performers-singers had been so successful in the United States, not to mention the rest of the world. It was so unique that they were aware that this was very, very special. Because, you know, with all of that stuff that went on in 1963—the fact that they'd broke the American market—I mean nobody had done that before.

Also, there were the influences that they knew about, like the Bob Dylan influence, the Beach Boys influence, and that kind of thing. But the bottom line I think was you can be aware of your influence, but you're also aware of *What is your next project?* I mean, the bottom line is, *Can you do it again?* So, it's a case of, the influence was there, they were aware of the influence, they were aware that they were famous, they were aware that the rest of the world was following them, but the bottom line was, *Can we keep this up? We've done* Sgt. Pepper's, *which changed the world, we had the fiasco in* Let It Be, *now can we do a proper album together, with* Abbey Road?

THOM: What I often take notice of is the experimentation at Abbey Road Studios during the 1960s. It seems particularly evident between 1966 and 1968 and seems to reflect a general interest in electro-acoustic music as manifest in the Cologne Studio and Radio France. What I was wondering was how aware were the Beatles, George Martin, and the other engineers like Geoff Emerick and Chris Thomas of the various aesthetic developments that were taking place in recorded sound?

PETER: I don't know because there was a situation where we never were at the recording studios, and I say we—Brian [Epstein] or myself were never there. I mean I would go there sometimes at the beginning of the sessions to discuss things with them that had to be decided—get things signed or get answers and everything, but we always left. And the only people in the studio would be the four Beatles, Neil Aspinall, Mal Evans, and the EMI staff—George and Geoff and whoever else. So, to try and answer your question, I don't know how aware they were, if they were at all. I think the difference, as you say, from 1966 onward is that when they stopped touring they had more time. So prior to 1966, albums were made between tours. They were squeezed in because there was a finite amount of time to produce them. Once they stopped touring, there was nothing else to do. There was no other call on their time except recording—and so there was the freedom of time so they could experiment more and this they took great advantage of. *Sgt. Pepper's* took forever to make—not by today's standards but by their standards.

THOM: It was a bit of a double-edged sword as well, wasn't it? They had quite a bit of time to experiment and to think about their music as art rather than just product. But at the same time, the fact that they no longer had to fit it in between touring, [this] created tensions that ultimately contributed to the breakup. Things became directionless, and McCartney was always trying to apply some kind of discipline or structure to the situation.

PETER: Yes, well, that, of course, was only accelerated by Brian's death. Although there was no question that Brian worried enormously once they were not touring because he felt that his contribution was lessened. And I think that was a needless worry, frankly. But I think most of what you say is actually what John was thinking about. I mean the fact that John had lost interest. John was kind of "antsy." Is that an American word?

THOM: Yes. [*laughter*]

PETER: Okay, and Paul, as you know, the moment Brian died, Paul said, "We must get on with life," and *Magical Mystery Tour* was the result, which was a mess, because Paul in his typical fashion wouldn't listen to anyone and just got on with, "Let's do something," which really was probably right but at the same time, it wasn't properly planned.

THOM: My research stresses a perceived frustration on the part of the mid-period Beatles with the limitations of conventional musical formats, for example, two-to-three-minute pop songs. Bearing this in mind, the entire late period (1967–1969) could be understood in terms of a journey toward the formal breakthrough that was the *Abbey Road* medley. Could you comment on the Beatles' attitude toward more conventional approaches to music composition?

PETER: I think that as an overall response to that is the fact that I think that they had this attitude—*we can do whatever we want to do*—and that *the restrictions that convention or that EMI recording company could put on us no longer apply. So if we want to have "A Day In The Life,"* which was . . . how many minutes long?

THOM: It was five-plus minutes . . .

PETER: Right, which was unthinkable—*but we can do it, and we can get away with it, and we will get away with it.* And so I think that it was an attitude that they could do whatever they want. From an academic point of view, that's not very detailed, but I mean that's sort of the attitude.

THOM: And as you pointed out earlier, they also had carte blanche as a result of their early success.

PETER: Yes.

THOM: The popular view of the construction of the *Abbey Road* album states that the impetus to create the medley came exclusively from George Martin and Paul McCartney. John Lennon has been quoted as saying that he disliked the "pop-suite" approach and instead preferred the individual song layout on side one of the *Abbey Road* album. However, in an interview from April 1969, Lennon describes how he and McCartney were planning a sequence of songs that would cover the entire side of an album.[1] He expresses an enthusiasm for the project that seems to belie the popular view.[2] Could you comment on this apparent discrepancy between public perception and private reality concerning the Beatles' creative dynamic?

PETER: I don't remember the circumstances of the interview, but my recollection is that there wasn't much cooperation at that point in time. Everyone was doing what they wanted to do, and, as usual, Paul was the doer—he was always the doer. He was the one that got on with stuff, and he was the one that would go into the studio and work with George Martin.

THOM: The interesting thing about that [interview] is that it suggests there was a period in early 1969 where Lennon and McCartney were intensely involved in the creation of the concept, which then ultimately was developed and brought to realization by McCartney and Martin.

PETER: I don't remember.

THOM: It's a very obscure interview. I've only found references to it in other sources. Typically, John Lennon is regarded as the literary specialist and rock 'n' roller of the Beatles, while Paul McCartney is considered the more natural musician and balladeer. Evidence suggests, however, that this categorization is far too facile to be true. For instance, Lennon wrote some of the group's most lyrical ballads, such as "Julia," "In My Life," and "If I Fell," while McCartney regularly produced hardedged material such as "I'm Down," "Birthday," and "Helter Skelter." Could you comment on this paradox and how it may have impacted on the recording of the *Abbey Road* album?

PETER: Well, I think probably they admired each other much more than they were willing to admit. And certainly I would think that John was more influenced by Paul than he was willing to admit, maybe even to himself. I think Paul always knew that some of his things were regarded by John as . . . [*pause*] the English word would be *naff*, meaning it's a little too commercial or too obvious like "Yesterday," or something like that. But I think that they had a profound respect for each other. And I think the problems sometimes were like with family—you grow apart slightly and maybe have a problem with personalities. But I think basically they had an enormous respect for each other, even though they may have had personality differences as they got older and lived separate lives—especially once Yoko appeared on the scene.

THOM: Do you sense a marked difference in perception concerning the Beatles and their achievements on this side of the Atlantic? When you speak with Americans does their perception contrast with the way the group is perceived in Britain?

PETER: No, I don't think so. I've never thought of it actually. Being a Brit who's lived in the United States for many years, I've always been aware that Americans are in general much more open and positive in their thinking than Europeans, who are much more cynical and questioning. I was in London this weekend and somebody said something and I said, "No, no, no . . . you missed the irony—we're in England." [*laughter*]

THOM: One of the things I notice is that we as Americans tend to define the Beatles in terms of an unknown quantity about their music. It's accepted that they were heavily influenced by American styles, but we also describe a magical quality that they brought to their creative work, which is often called the "British-ness" of it. I often wonder if there are things we're missing in their style, such as influences from people who are not known here, like George Formby.

PETER: Yeah, I think that the only thing I can say about that is that it's not the British-ness; it's the Liverpool-ness, because Liverpool has always been a bit different—George Formby was a Liverpudlian. Liverpool was a very, very successful port, I mean up until our period. Earlier in the twentieth century, it had been the largest port in Britain. It was immensely rich because all of the raw commodities from the

British Empire like wool and cotton, which came through this port, were manufactured in the north of England, and were then exported again. Also, the passenger liners, in those days, went from Liverpool, not from Southhampton. It was an amazingly successful English port. As the twentieth century went on, it became less and less so. And in our day, in the 1950s and 1960s, it was struggling a bit. But there was always an arrogance about the working class Liverpudlians like, "Fuck you," you know, "we'll manage on our own." And it was like the old story that a lot of comedians came from Liverpool, but you had to be a comedian to come from Liverpool. So there was always an attitude about Liverpudlians, and I think that the Beatles, because they came from that culture, and then at a very early age had to go and survive in Hamburg (where it was a question of survival), they learned to be very independent, and that attitude became their thing. But I don't think it's a British thing; I think it's a Liverpool thing. And it seemed to work well with their quick minds and their wit, but I think it was definitely a Liverpool thing.

Also, the other thing about Liverpool was the fact that there was a lot of knowledge about American music that wasn't available in the rest of the country because of the sailors. A lot of the young, working-class boys would go to sea initially. They would start going into the Merchant Marines when they were sixteen, seventeen, eighteen years old. And they would go to sea to make some money. And, of course, a lot of those would go to America, and they would spend time in America, they would buy American records, because in those days, of course, the radio in Britain was very restrictive, and there wasn't much going on. So we in Liverpool, and in the record stores that Brian [Epstein] and I worked in, were much more sophisticated about American music than probably the rest of the country.

THOM: Having two grandparents who came from Scotland, I grew up in a house that was dominated by British culture. As a result, I always recognized a quality in the Beatles' humor and attitude that seemed very familiar. I noticed in the course of my research that McCartney and Lennon both had relatives from Scotland and Ireland. Has the city's immigrant population contributed to the distinctive Liverpool attitude you described?

PETER: Well, of course there is a very large Irish population, which is traditionally the underdog and is always having to fight for survival. In Liverpool, the other thing that they had was, because there was such a large Irish population, which was Catholic, there was also the indigenous Protestant population, and there was always a conflict between the two. Liverpool had two soccer teams, Liverpool and Everton. Everton is a part of Liverpool, and the Protestants used to support one team, and the Catholics used to support the other—two very different groups. I don't know about George, but I think that Ringo, John, and Paul all had some Irish ancestry.

THOM: There's been some writing on the Beatles that discusses the relationship between John and Paul, the creative dynamic between them from the time they met, as being the thing that ultimately becomes the Beatles. Do you find that to be accurate in your experience?

PETER: Not necessarily. I mean I think that's certainly part of it, but I think George had a very significant role to play, and they listened to him. He was the youngest, of course, so he was always considered not quite as equal as the others, which of course riled him. And Ringo, of course, was the last to arrive. So, there was a balance, and I think it was very important, especially as they developed. I think Ringo was very important in that perception. I don't know how much you'd want to ascribe to him in the studio, but as a group and in the way they dealt with the world they were all very important. The smart-ass answers came from all of them.

THOM: Ringo's wit also seemed to contribute greatly to their lyrical content.

PETER: Yes, and George was pretty good, too.

THOM: Absolutely. Well, that's basically what I came to learn about. I was wondering if you could suggest some other avenues of research that I might explore in relation to the topic.

PETER: The *Abbey Road* album?

THOM: Yes.

PETER: The only thing is the miracle that it ever happened at all. And I don't quite know why it happened. I think it may have been just that the bad blood that had happened with *Let It Be* had softened, and there was a will to do something that made it happen. But it is amazing that it did get done.

THOM: In the *Anthology*, there's an interview with Ringo where he speculates on what many people seem to feel—that is, that they could have gone on and done another album or they could have found another way to work where they might have done some solo projects and then always come back and work in the studio together. Do you think that was a possibility?

PETER: Yeah, I do. I think it was only the fact that John wasn't willing to go along with that, and it got really nasty that it became impossible. But I think, yes, if that hadn't happened they could easily had done that and continued to do that, but John didn't want to do it. And I think he got himself in a situation where there was no going back, which was encouraged by Yoko.

THOM: You mentioned George earlier, and I think one of the realities of the late Beatles is that he was emerging as a songwriter, and, of course, on *Abbey Road*, although it's not quite three equal songwriters, he's certainly a major force on the album. Some have speculated that John might not have been able to tolerate that.

PETER: Well, I don't know if that was so, because, first of all, John and George were pretty good friends, and I don't think John was scared of much. I think that if he'd had a problem he would have dealt with it. He wasn't one to be quiet about anything. And of course when the mess came, George and Ringo got behind him—a mistake, but still . . .

THOM: As musicians, we always recognized how important and influential the Beatles were, and a considerable part of my early adult life was spent trying to present evidence so as to say, "Look, they [the Beatles] are doing things that are significant, so let's acknowledge this." And of course there was an attitude that was something like, "Well, they're good for pop." But based on the evidence, there was a sense that this might be more significant with regard to the ongoing tradition of music composition. It's gotten to a point now where, on the one hand, people accept it so that I don't have to justify it anymore because everyone recognizes it, and on the other hand, there's a sense that they're quite a bit bigger than we initially realized—that this may be quite a bit more important. As we get farther away from it, we begin to see that this may well be a major moment in musical history. Do you get that sense based on your experience?

PETER: Yeah, and I think that when it came home to me was when the *Number One* CD went to something like twenty million in sales worldwide, and one thinks, "Where the fuck did that all come from?" Because it wasn't us rebuying our old CDs, and it wasn't our children buying it. It was a new audience of kids discovering it on their own. And they weren't buying these CDs because their parents told them to, because that's not how it works. This was a whole new audience. My contemporaries now tell me about how their children or grandchildren have discovered, somehow or other—I don't know how they do this—have discovered the Beatles. It seems to be extraordinary that whatever is there has not gotten old. And however you describe the influence, it has a hook, which is still relevant. There's been nothing quite like it since.

But then of course from your point of view there's the fact that you've got four people who were terribly uneducated in musical structure—this was all innate talent. And I remember the famous case of William Mann, you know, of the *London Times* when he analyzed, you know, whatever it was . . . *Abbey Road* or, not *Abbey Road*, "Penny Lane" or . . . no, no I don't remember what it was.

THOM: As I recall, it was following the release of *With the Beatles*, and the article mentions the song "Not a Second Time."

PETER: Yes, and I knew him—we met him subsequently. But I mean this man was not a *bullshitter*; this man was not trying to climb on a bandwagon; this man was not trying to be *smart-assed* or trying to show that he'd found something that nobody else had found. This man was a very serious, open-minded person, so it was very interesting that he'd noticed. Also, George Martin's influence, I think, was immense—the Bach trumpet on "Penny Lane" and that kind of thing. And the fact that they had somebody as a producer who was so knowledgeable and so low-key, but *influential* and low-key so he didn't push his ideas on these uneducated guys, but was supportive and was just a *nice guy* who happened to know a lot more about music than they did and was willing to go along with them—so that was luck.

THOM: It's interesting that the William Mann article you mentioned was often the subject of jokes within the group and without. He describes the aeolian cadences close "Not a Second Time" as being particularly significant. This prompted Lennon to comment, "I have no idea what they are. . . . they sound like exotic birds." Today, however, Mann's observations not only seem extremely apt, they also sit very well within the body of serious scholarship.

PETER: Yes. I think the argument is, How educated should you be? Or does the education destroy your natural talent, or *can* it destroy some of your natural talent?

THOM: . . . to do it instinctively instead.

PETER: Right.

THOM: Well, thank you very much for your time. It's been a great pleasure.

PETER: You're very welcome.

NOTES

1. The interview described is from the *New Musical Express*, April 1969. Lennon: "Paul and I are now working on a kind of song montage that we might do as one piece on one side. We've got about two weeks to finish the whole thing, so we're really working at it." Peter Doggett, *Let It Be/Abbey Road: The Beatles* (New York and London: Schirmer Books/Prentice Hall International, 1998), 49.

2. In his book *Summer of Love* (1994) producer George Martin commented on this very point: "By the time we came to do *Abbey Road*, the madness years were over, and John was happy to help us with the second side of the album: he wrote quite a bit of it! 'Because' is one of his masterpieces." Martin and Pearson, *Summer of Love*, 140.

APPENDIX C: DISCOGRAPHY

THE BEATLES' BRITISH ALBUMS, EPs, AND SINGLES (1962–1970)

Albums

LP: *Please Please Me*
(released: 22.03.1963 [UK] on Parlophone PMC 1201 [mono]; released: 26.04.1963 [UK] on Parlophone PCS 3042 [stereo])

1. I Saw Her Standing There
2. Misery
3. Anna (Go to Him)
4. Chains
5. Boys
6. Ask Me Why
7. Please Please Me
8. Love Me Do
9. P.S. I Love You
10. Baby It's You
11. Do You Want to Know a Secret

    12. A Taste of Honey
    13. There's A Place
    14. Twist and Shout[1]

LP: *With the Beatles*
  (released: 22.11.1963 [UK] on Parlophone PMC 1206 [mono]; Parlophone PCS 3045 [stereo])

    1. It Won't Be Long
    2. All I've Got to Do
    3. All My Loving
    4. Don't Bother Me
    5. Little Child
    6. Till There Was You
    7. Please Mister Postman
    8. Roll Over Beethoven
    9. Hold Me Tight
   10. You Really Got a Hold on Me
   11. I Wanna Be Your Man
   12. Devil in Her Heart
   13. Not a Second Time
   14. Money (That's What I Want)[2]

LP: *A Hard Day's Night*
  (released: 10.07.1964 [UK] on Parlophone PMC 1230 [mono]; Parlophone PCS 3058 [stereo])

    1. A Hard Day's Night
    2. I Should Have Known Better
    3. If I Fell
    4. I'm Happy Just to Dance with You
    5. And I Love Her
    6. Tell Me Why
    7. Can't Buy Me Love
    8. Any Time at All
    9. I'll Cry Instead

10. Things We Said Today
11. When I Get Home
12. You Can't Do That
13. I'll Be Back[3]

LP: *Beatles for Sale*
    (released: 04.12.1964 [UK] on Parlophone PMC 1240 [mono]; Parlophone PCS 3062 [stereo])

1. No Reply
2. I'm a Loser
3. Baby's in Black
4. Rock and Roll Music
5. I'll Follow the Sun
6. Mr. Moonlight
7. Kansas City—Hey, Hey, Hey, Hey
8. Eight Days a Week
9. Words of Love
10. Honey Don't
11. Every Little Thing
12. I Don't Want to Spoil the Party
13. What You're Doing
14. Everybody's Trying to Be My Baby[4]

LP: *Help!*
    (released: 06.08.1965 [UK] on Parlophone PMC 1255 [mono]; Parlophone PCS 3071 [stereo])

1. Help!
2. The Night Before
3. You've Got to Hide Your Love Away
4. I Need You
5. Another Girl
6. You're Going to Lose That Girl
7. Ticket to Ride
8. Act Naturally

9. It's Only Love
10. You Like Me Too Much
11. Tell Me What You See
12. I've Just Seen a Face
13. Yesterday
14. Dizzy Miss Lizzy[5]

LP: *Rubber Soul*
(released: 03.12.1965 [UK] on Parlophone PMC 1267 [mono]; Parlophone PCS 3075 [stereo])

1. Drive My Car
2. Norwegian Wood (This Bird Has Flown)
3. You Won't See Me
4. Nowhere Man
5. Think for Yourself
6. The Word
7. Michelle
8. What Goes On
9. Girl
10. I'm Looking Through You
11. In My Life
12. Wait
13. If I Needed Someone
14. Run for Your Life[6]

LP: *Revolver*
(released: 05.08.1966 [UK] on Parlophone PMC 7009 [mono]; Parlophone PCS 7009 [stereo])

1. Taxman
2. Eleanor Rigby
3. I'm Only Sleeping
4. Love You To
5. Here, There, and Everywhere
6. Yellow Submarine
7. She Said She Said

8. Good Day Sunshine
9. And Your Bird Can Sing
10. For No One
11. Doctor Robert
12. I Want to Tell You
13. Got to Get You into My Life
14. Tomorrow Never Knows[7]

LP: *Sgt. Pepper's Lonely Hearts Club Band*
(released: 01.06.1967 [UK] on Parlophone PMC 7027 [mono]; Parlophone PCS 7027 [stereo])

1. Sgt. Pepper's Lonely Hearts Club Band
2. With a Little Help from My Friends
3. Lucy in the Sky with Diamonds
4. Getting Better
5. Fixing a Hole
6. She's Leaving Home
7. Being for the Benefit of Mr. Kite
8. Within You Without You
9. When I'm Sixty-Four
10. Lovely Rita
11. Good Morning, Good Morning
12. Sgt. Pepper's Lonely Hearts Club Band (Reprise)
13. A Day in the Life[8]

LP: *The Beatles* [*White Album*]
(released: 22.11.1968 [UK] on Parlophone PMC 7067–7068 [mono]; Parlophone PCS 7067–7068 [stereo])

1. Back in the USSR
2. Dear Prudence
3. Glass Onion
4. Ob-La-Di, Ob-La-Da
5. Wild Honey Pie
6. The Continuing Story of Bungalow Bill

   7. While My Guitar Gently Weeps
   8. Happiness Is a Warm Gun
   9. Martha My Dear
 10. I'm So Tired
 11. Blackbird
 12. Piggies
 13. Rocky Raccoon
 14. Don't Pass Me By
 15. Why Don't We Do It in the Road
 16. I Will
 17. Julia
 18. Birthday
 19. Yer Blues
 20. Mother Nature's Son
 21. Everybody's Got Something to Hide Except for Me and My Monkey
 22. Sexy Sadie
 23. Helter Skelter
 24. Long, Long, Long
 25. Revolution (1)
 26. Honey Pie
 27. Savoy Truffle
 28. Cry Baby Cry
 29. Revolution #9
 30. Good Night[9]

LP: *Yellow Submarine*
(released: 17.01.1969 on Parlophone PMC 7070 [mono]; Parlophone PCS 7070 [stereo])

 1. Yellow Submarine
 2. Only a Northern Song
 3. All Together Now
 4. Hey Bulldog
 5. It's All Too Much
 6. All You Need Is Love[10]

LP: *Abbey Road*
(released: 26.09.1969 on [UK] Parlophone PCS 7088 [stereo only])

1. Come Together
2. Something
3. Maxwell's Silver Hammer
4. Oh! Darling
5. Octopus's Garden
6. I Want You (She's So Heavy)
7. Here Comes the Sun
8. Because
9. You Never Give Me Your Money
10. Sun King
11. Mean Mr. Mustard
12. Polythene Pam
13. She Came in Through the Bathroom Window
14. Golden Slumbers
15. Carry That Weight
16. The End
17. Her Majesty[11]

LP: *Let It Be*
(released: 08.05.1970 [UK] on Apple/Parlophone PCS 7096 [stereo only])

1. Two of Us
2. Dig a Pony
3. Across the Universe
4. I Me Mine
5. Dig It
6. Let It Be
7. Maggie Mae
8. I've Got a Feeling
9. One after 909
10. The Long and Winding Road
11. For You Blue
12. Get Back[12]

EPs

Long Tall Sally
(released: 19.06.1964 [UK] on Parlophone GEP 8913)

1. Long Tall Sally
2. I Call Your Name
3. Slow Down
4. Matchbox[13]

Magical Mystery Tour
(released: 08.12.1967 [UK] on Parlophone MMT-1 [mono] and SMMT-1 [stereo])

1. Magical Mystery Tour
2. The Fool on the Hill
3. Flying
4. Blue Jay Way[14]
5. Your Mother Should Know
6. I Am the Walrus

Singles

1. Love Me Do (released: 05.10.1962 [UK] on Parlophone 45-R 4949)

   - A-Side: Love Me Do
   - B-Side: P.S. I Love You[15]

2. Please Please Me (released: 11.01.1963 [UK] on Parlophone 45-R 4983)

   - A-Side: Please Please Me
   - B-Side: Ask Me Why[16]

3. From Me to You (released: 11.04.1963 [UK] on Parlophone R 5015)

   - A-Side: From Me to You
   - B-Side: Thank You Girl[17]

4. She Loves You (released: 23.08.1963 [UK] on Parlophone R 5055)

- A-Side: She Loves You
- B-Side: I'll Get You[18]

5. I Want to Hold Your Hand (released: 29.11.1963 [UK] on Parlophone R 5084)

- A-Side: I Want to Hold Your Hand
- B-Side: This Boy[19]

6. Can't Buy Me Love (released: 20.03.1964 [UK] on Parlophone R 5114)

- A-Side: Can't Buy Me Love
- B-Side: You Can't Do That[20]

7. A Hard Day's Night (released: 10.07.1964 [UK] on Parlophone R 5160)

- A-Side: A Hard Day's Night
- B-Side: Things We Said Today[21]

8. I Feel Fine (released: 27.11.1964 [UK] on Parlophone R 5200)

- A-Side: I Feel Fine
- B-Side: She's a Woman[22]

9. Ticket to Ride (released: 09.04.1965 [UK] on Parlophone R 5265)

- A-Side: Ticket to Ride
- B-Side: Yes It Is[23]

10. Help! (released: 23.07.1965 [UK] on Parlophone R 5305)

- A-Side: Help!
- B-Side: I'm Down[24]

11. We Can Work It Out (released: 03.12.1965 [UK] on Parlophone R 5389)

- We Can Work It Out
- Day Tripper[25]

12. Paperback Writer (released: 10.06.1966 [UK] on Parlophone R 5452)

   - Paperback Writer
   - Rain[26]

13. Eleanor Rigby (released: 05.08.1966 [UK] on Parlophone R 5493)

   - Eleanor Rigby
   - Yellow Submarine[27]

14. Strawberry Fields Forever (released: 17.02.1967 [UK] on Parlophone R 5570)

   - Strawberry Fields Forever
   - Penny Lane[28]

15. All You Need Is Love (released: 07.07.1967 [UK] on Parlophone R 5620; the title song was aired on the Eurovision program "Our World" on 25.06.1967)

   - A-Side: All You Need Is Love
   - B-Side: Baby You're a Rich Man[29]

16. Hello Goodbye (released: 24.11.1967 [UK] on Parlophone R 5655)

   - A-Side: Hello Goodbye
   - B-Side: I Am the Walrus[30]

17. Lady Madonna (released: 15.03.1968 [UK] on Parlophone R 5675)

   - A-Side: Lady Madonna
   - B-Side: The Inner Light[31]

18. Hey Jude (released: 30.08.1968 [UK] on Apple [Parlophone] R 5722)

   - A-Side: Hey Jude
   - B-Side: Revolution[32]

19. Get Back (released: 11.04.1969 [UK] on Apple [Parlophone] R 5777)

  - A-Side: Get Back (with Billy Preston on piano)
  - B-Side: Don't Let Me Down (with Billy Preston on piano)[33]

20. The Ballad of John and Yoko (released: 30.05.1969 [UK] on Apple [Parlophone] R 5786)

  - A-Side: The Ballad of John and Yoko
  - B-Side: Old Brown Shoe[34]

21. Something (released: 31.10.1969 [UK] on Apple [Parlophone] R 5814)

  - A-Side: Something
  - B-Side: Come Together[35]

22. Let It Be (released: 06.03.1970 [UK] on Apple [Parlophone] R 5833)

  - A-Side: Let It Be (with Billy Preston on piano)
  - B-Side: You Know My Name (Look Up the Number)[36]

ADDITIONAL RECORDED WORKS THAT ARE REFERENCED IN THE TEXT (LISTED IN CHRONOLOGICAL ORDER)

LP: The Beach Boys, *Pet Sounds* (Capitol 2458), 1966[37]

1. Wouldn't It Be Nice
2. You Still Believe in Me
3. That's Not Me
4. Don't Talk (Put Your Head on My Shoulder)
5. I'm Waiting for the Day
6. Let's Go Away for Awhile

7. Sloop John B
8. God Only Knows
9. I Know There's an Answer
10. Here Today
11. I Just Wasn't Made for These Times
12. Pet Sounds
13. Caroline, No

45rpm: Beach Boys, *Good Vibrations/Wendy* (Capitol 15475), 1966[38]

LP: The Beatles, *The Beatles' Christmas Album* (Apple LYN 2154), 1970[39]

1. 1963: The Beatles' Christmas Record
2. 1964: Another Beatles Christmas Record
3. 1965: The Beatles' Third Christmas Record
4. 1966: Pantomime: Everywhere It's Christmas
5. 1967: Christmas Time Is Here Again
6. 1968: Happy Christmas 1968
7. 1969: Happy Christmas 1969

LP: McCartney, Paul & Linda: *Ram* (Apple PAS 10003), 1971[40]

1. Too Many People
2. 3 Legs
3. Ram On
4. Dear Boy
5. Uncle Albert/Admiral Halsey
6. Smile Away
7. Heart of the Country
8. Monkberry Moon Delight
9. Eat at Home
10. Long Haired Lady
11. Ram On
12. The Back Seat of My Car

LP: Paul McCartney & Wings: *Red Rose Speedway* (Apple PCTC 251), 1973[41]

1. Big Barn Bed
2. My Love
3. Get on the Right Thing
4. One More Kiss
5. Little Lamb Dragonfly
6. Single Pigeon
7. When the Night
8. Loup (1st Indian on the Moon)
9. Medley: Hold Me Tight/Lazy Dynamite/Hands of Love/Power Cut

LP: Wings, *Band on the Run* (Apple PAS 10007), 1973[42]

1. Band on the Run
2. Jet
3. Bluebird
4. Mrs. Vandebilt
5. Let Me Roll It
6. Mamunia
7. No Words
8. Helen Wheels
9. Picasso's Last Words (Drink to Me)
10. Nineteen Hundred and Eighty Five

LP: Pink Floyd, *The Dark Side of the Moon* (Harvest 11163), 1973[43]

1. Speak to Me/Breathe in the Air
2. On the Run
3. Time
4. The Great Gig in the Sky
5. Money
6. Us and Them
7. Any Colour You Like

8. Brain Damage
9. Eclipse

LP: Billy Joel, *The Stranger* (Columbia 34987) 1977[44]

1. Movin' Out (Anthony's Song)
2. The Stranger
3. Just the Way You Are
4. Scenes from an Italian Restaurant
5. Vienna
6. Only the Good Die Young
7. She's Always a Woman
8. Get It Right the First Time
9. Everybody Has a Dream

LP: Wings, *Back to the Egg* (Parlophone PCTC 257), 1979[45]

1. Reception
2. Getting Closer
3. We're Open Tonight
4. Spin It On
5. Again and Again and Again
6. Old Siam, Sir
7. Arrow Through Me
8. Rockestra Theme
9. To You
10. After the Ball/Million Miles
11. Winter Rose/Love Awake
12. The Broadcast
13. So Glad to See You Here
14. Baby's Request

CD: Paul McCartney, *Liverpool Oratorio* (EMI 54371 [2]), 1991[46]

Disc 1

1. Liverpool Oratorio: Movement I—War: Andante (Orchestra)
2. Liverpool Oratorio: Movement I—War: "Non nobis solum"

3. Liverpool Oratorio: Movement I—War: "The Air Raid Siren Slices Through . . ." (Shanty)
4. Liverpool Oratorio: Movement I—War: "Oh Will It All End Here?" (Shanty)
5. Liverpool Oratorio: Movement I—War: "Mother and Father Holding Their Child"
6. Liverpool Oratorio: Movement II—School: "We're Here in School Today to Get a Perfect Education"
7. Liverpool Oratorio: Movement II—School: "Walk in Single File out of the Classroom" (Headmaster)
8. Liverpool Oratorio: Movement II—School: "Settle Down"
9. Liverpool Oratorio: Movement II—School: "Kept in Confusion" (Shanty)
10. Liverpool Oratorio: Movement II—School: "I'll Always Be Here" (Mary Dee)
11. Liverpool Oratorio: Movement II—School: "Boys, This Is Your Teacher" (Headmaster, Miss Inkley)
12. Liverpool Oratorio: Movement II—School: "Tres conejos" (Miss Inkley, Headmaster, Shanty)
13. Liverpool Oratorio: Movement II—School: "Not for Ourselves" (Headmaster, Miss Inkley, Shanty)
14. Liverpool Oratorio: Movement III—Crypt: "And So It Was That I Had Grown" (Shanty)
15. Liverpool Oratorio: Movement III—Crypt: Dance
16. Liverpool Oratorio: Movement III—Crypt: "I Used to Come Here When This Place Was a Crypt" (Shanty, Preacher)
17. Liverpool Oratorio: Movement III—Crypt: "Here Now" (Shanty)
18. Liverpool Oratorio: Movement III—Crypt: "I'll Always Be Here" (Mary Dee, Shanty)
19. Liverpool Oratorio: Movement III—Crypt: "Now's the Time to Tell Him" (Mary Dee, Shanty)
20. Liverpool Oratorio: Movement IV—Father: Andante Lamentoso
21. Liverpool Oratorio: Movement IV—Father: "O Father, You Have Given . . ." (Chief Mourner)
22. Liverpool Oratorio: Movement IV—Father: "(Ah)"
23. Liverpool Oratorio: Movement IV—Father: "Hey, Wait a Minute" (Shanty)

24. Liverpool Oratorio: Movement IV—Father: "Father, Father, Father" (Shanty, Chief Mourner)

Disc 2

1. Liverpool Oratorio: Movement V—Wedding: Andante Amoroso—"Know I Should Be Glad of This" (Shanty, Mary Dee)
2. Liverpool Oratorio: Movement V—Wedding: "Father, Hear Our Humble Voices" (Preacher)
3. Liverpool Oratorio: Movement V—Wedding ("Hosanna, Hosanna") (Mary Dee, Shanty)
4. Liverpool Oratorio: Movement VI—Work: Allegro Energico
5. Liverpool Oratorio: Movement VI—Work: "Working Women at the Top" (Mary Dee)
6. Liverpool Oratorio: Movement VI—Work: Violin Solo
7. Liverpool Oratorio: Movement VI—Work: "Did I Sign the Letter . . ." (Mary Dee)
8. Liverpool Oratorio: Movement VI—Work: Tempo I
9. Liverpool Oratorio: Movement VI—Work: "When You Ask a Working Man" (Shanty, Mr. Dingle)
10. Liverpool Oratorio: Movement VI—Work: "Let's Find Ourselves a Little Hostelry" (Mr. Dingle)
11. Liverpool Oratorio: Movement VII—Crises: Allegro Molto
12. Liverpool Oratorio: Movement VII—Crises: "The World You're Coming Into" (Mary Dee)
13. Liverpool Oratorio: Movement VII—Crises: Tempo I
14. Liverpool Oratorio: Movement VII—Crises: "Where's My Dinner?" (Shanty, Mary Dee)
15. Liverpool Oratorio: Movement VII—Crises: "Let's Not Argue" (Shanty, Mary Dee)
16. Liverpool Oratorio: Movement VII—Crises: "I'm Not a Slave" (Mary Dee, Shanty)
17. Liverpool Oratorio: Movement VII—Crises: "Right! That's It!" (Mary Dee)
18. Liverpool Oratorio: Movement VII—Crises: "Stop. Wait."

19. Liverpool Oratorio: Movement VII—Crises: "Do You Know Who You Are . . ." (Nurse)
20. Liverpool Oratorio: Movement VII—Crises: "Ghosts of the Past Left Behind" (Nurse, Shanty, Mary Dee)
21. Liverpool Oratorio: Movement VII—Crises: "Do We Live in a World . . ." (Mary Dee, Nurse, Shanty)
22. Liverpool Oratorio: Movement VIII—Peace: "And So It Was That You Were Born" (Shanty)
23. Liverpool Oratorio: Movement VIII—Peace: "God Is Good"
24. Liverpool Oratorio: Movement VIII—Peace: "What People Want Is a Family Life" (Preacher)
25. Liverpool Oratorio: Movement VIII—Peace: "Dad's in the Garden" (Nurse, Mary Dee, Preacher, Shanty)
26. Liverpool Oratorio: Movement VIII—Peace: "So On and On the Story Goes" (Shanty, Mary Dee)[47]

CD: Rundgren, Todd, *No World Order* (Rhino R2/R4 71266), 1993[48]

1. Worldwide Epiphany
2. No World Order
3. Worldwide Epiphany
4. Day Job
5. Property
6. Fascist Christ
7. Love Thing
8. Time Stood Still
9. Proactivity
10. No World Order
11. World Epiphany
12. Time Stood Still
13. Love Thing
14. Time Stood Still
15. Word Made Flesh
16. Fever Broke

CD: The Beatles, *Anthology 1* (Apple PCSP 727), 1995.[49]

Disc 1

1. Free as a Bird
2. We Were Four Guys . . . That's All (John Lennon speaking to Jann Wenner of *Rolling Stone* 8 December 1970, New York City)
3. That'll Be the Day (Phillips Sound Recording Service, Liverpool, 1958)
4. In Spite of All the Danger (Phillips Sound Recording Service, Liverpool, 1958)
5. Sometimes I'd Borrow . . . Those Still Exist (Paul McCartney speaking to Mark Lewisohn, 3 November 1994, London)
6. Hallelujah, I Love Her So
7. You'll Be Mine
8. Cayenne
9. First of All . . . It Didn't Do a Thing Here (Paul McCartney speaking to Malcolm Threadgill. Recorded 27 October 1962, Hulme Hall, Port Sunlight, Cheshire)
10. My Bonnie (Friederich-Ebert-Halle, Hamburg, 22 June 1961)
11. Ain't She Sweet (Friederich-Ebert-Halle, Hamburg, 22 June 1961)
12. Cry for a Shadow (Friederich-Ebert-Halle, Hamburg, 22 June 1961)
13. "Brian was a beautiful guy . . . he presented us well" (John Lennon speaking to David Wigg. October 1971, New York City)
14. "I secured them . . . a Beatle drink even then" (Brian Epstein reading an extract from his autobiography, *A Cellarful of Noise*)
15. Searchin' (Decca Studios, London, 1 January 1962)
16. Three Cool Cats (Decca Studios, London, 1 January 1962)
17. The Sheik of Araby (Decca Studios, London, 1 January 1962)
18. Like Dreamers Do (Decca Studios, London, 1 January 1962)
19. Hello Little Girl (Decca Studios, London, 1 January 1962)
20. "Well, the recording test . . . by my artists" (Brian Epstein reading an extract from his autobiography, *A Cellarful of Noise*)
21. Besame Mucho (EMI Studios, London, 6 June 1962)
22. Love Me Do (EMI Studios, London, 6 June 1962)
23. How Do You Do It? (EMI Studios, London, 4 September 1962)
24. Please Please Me (early take)

25. One After 909 (sequence)
26. One After 909 (complete)
27. Lend Me Your Comb (BBC Maida Vale Studios, London, 2 July 1963)
28. I'll Get You (London Palladium, 13 October 1963)
29. "We were performers . . . in Britain" (John Lennon speaking to Jann Wenner of *Rolling Stone*, 8 December 1970, New York City)
30. I Saw Her Standing There (Karlaplansstudion, Stockholm, 24 October 1963)
31. From Me to You (Karlaplansstudion, Stockholm, 24 October 1963)
32. Money (That's What I Want) (Karlaplansstudion, Stockholm, 24 October 1963)
33. You Really Got a Hold on Me (Karlaplansstudion, Stockholm, 24 October 1963)
34. Roll over Beethoven (Karlaplansstudion, Stockholm, 24 October 1963)

Disc 2

1. She Loves You (Prince of Wales Theatre, London, 4 November 1963)
2. Till There Was You (Prince of Wales Theatre, London, 4 November 1963)
3. Twist and Shout (Prince of Wales Theatre, London, 4 November 1963)
4. This Boy (ATV Studios, Borehamwood, 2 December 1963)
5. I Want to Hold Your Hand (ATV Studios, Borehamwood, 2 December 1963)
6. "Boys, what I was thinking" (comedy skit with Eric Morecambe and Ernie Wise—ATV Studios, Borehamwood, 2 December 1963)
7. Moonlight Bay (with Eric Morecambe and Ernie Wise—ATV Studios, Borehamwood, 2 December 1963)
8. Can't Buy Me Love (take 2)
9. All My Loving (The Ed Sullivan Show, 9 February 1964)
10. You Can't Do That (take 6)
11. And I Love Her (take 2)
12. A Hard Day's Night (take 1)

13. I Wanna Be Your Man (Recording session for *Around the Beatles,* 19 April 1964)
14. Long Tall Sally (Recording session for *Around the Beatles,* 19 April 1964)
15. Boys (Recording session for *Around the Beatles,* 19 April 1964)
16. Shout (Recording session for *Around the Beatles,* 19 April 1964)
17. I'll Be Back (take 2)
18. I'll Be Back (take 3)
19. You Know What to Do (previously unreleased George Harrison composition)
20. No Reply (demo)
21. Mr. Moonlight (composite of takes 1 and 4)
22. Leave My Kitten Alone
23. No Reply (take 2)
24. Eight Days a Week (sequence)
25. Eight Days a Week (complete)
26. Kansas City/Hey-Hey-Hey-Hey! (take 2)

CD: The Beatles, *Anthology 2* (Apple PCSP 728), 1996[50]

Disc 1

1. Real Love
2. Yes It Is (composite of various takes)
3. I'm Down (take 1)
4. You've Got to Hide Your Love Away (take 5)
5. If You've Got Trouble (previously unreleased Lennon-McCartney composition)
6. That Means A Lot (take 1)
7. Yesterday (take 1)
8. It's Only Love (take 2)
9. I Feel Fine (from *Blackpool Night Out,* 1 August 1965)
10. Ticket to Ride (from *Blackpool Night Out,* 1 August 1965)
11. Yesterday (from *Blackpool Night Out,* 1 August 1965)
12. Help! (from *Blackpool Night Out,* 1 August 1965)
13. Everybody's Trying to Be My Baby (*Shea Stadium,* New York, 15 August 1965)

14. Norwegian Wood (This Bird Has Flown) (take 1)
15. I'm Looking Through You (version 1)
16. 12-Bar Original (previously unreleased)
17. Tomorrow Never Knows (take 1)
18. Got to Get You into My Life (take 5)
19. And Your Bird Can Sing (version 1)
20. Taxman (take 11)
21. Eleanor Rigby (strings only)
22. I'm Only Sleeping (rehearsal)
23. I'm Only Sleeping (take 1)
24. Rock and Roll Music (Nippon Budokan Hall, Tokyo, 30 June 1966)
25. She's a Woman (Nippon Budokan Hall, Tokyo, 30 June 1966)

Disc 2

1. Strawberry Fields Forever (demo sequence)
2. Strawberry Fields Forever (take 1)
3. Strawberry Fields Forever (take 7 and edit piece)
4. Penny Lane (composite mix)
5. A Day in the Life (composite mix)
6. Good Morning Good Morning (Take 8)
7. Only a Northern Song
8. Being for the Benefit of Mr. Kite! (takes 1 and 2)
9. Being for the Benefit of Mr. Kite! (take 7)
10. Lucy in the Sky with Diamonds (composite mix)
11. Within You Without You (instrumental)
12. Sgt. Pepper's Lonely Hearts Club Band (reprise) (take 5)
13. You Know My Name (Look up the Number) (unedited)
14. I Am the Walrus (take 16)
15. The Fool on the Hill (demo)
16. Your Mother Should Know (take 27)
17. The Fool on the Hill (take 4)
18. Hello, Goodbye (take 16)
19. Lady Madonna (composite mix)
20. Across the Universe (take 2)

CD: The Beatles, *Anthology 3* (Apple PCSP 729), 1996[51]

Disc 1

1. A Beginning (previously unreleased)
2. Happiness Is a Warm Gun (Esher demo)
3. Helter Skelter (take 2)
4. Mean Mr. Mustard (Esher demo)
5. Polythene Pam (Esher demo)
6. Glass Onion (Esher demo)
7. Junk (Esher demo)
8. Piggies (Esher demo)
9. Honey Pie (Esher demo)
10. Don't Pass Me By (Composite mix)
11. Ob-La-Di, Ob-La-Da (version 1)
12. Good Night (composite mix)
13. Cry Baby Cry (take 1)
14. Blackbird (take 4)
15. Sexy Sadie (take 6)
16. While My Guitar Gently Weeps (take 1)
17. Hey Jude (rehearsal)
18. Not Guilty (take 102)
19. Mother Nature's Son (take 20)
20. Glass Onion (alternate mono mix)
21. Rocky Raccoon (Take 8)
22. What's the New Mary Jane (take 4)
23. Step Inside Love/Los Paranoias (outtakes from sessions for "I Will")
24. I'm So Tired (composite mix)
25. I Will (take 1)
26. Why Don't We Do It in the Road (take 4)
27. Julia (take 2)

Disc 2

1. I've Got a Feeling (Apple Studios, London, 23 January 1969)
2. She Came in Through the Bathroom Window (Apple Studios, London, 22 January 1969)

3. Dig a Pony (Apple Studios, London, 22 January 1969)
4. Two of Us (Apple Studios, London, 24 January 1969)
5. For You Blue (Apple Studios, London, 25 January 1969)
6. Teddy Boy (Apple Studios, London, 24 and 28 January 1969)
7. Medley: Rip It Up/Shake Rattle and Roll/Blue Suede Shoes (Apple Studios, London, 26 January 1969)
8. The Long and Winding Road (Apple Studios, London, 26 January 1969)
9. Oh! Darling (Apple Studios, London, 27 January 1969)
10. All Things Must Pass (demo)
11. Mailman, Bring Me No More Blues (Apple Studios, London, 29 January 1969)
12. Get Back (Apple (roof), London, 26 January 1969)
13. Old Brown Shoe (demo)
14. Octopus's Garden (take 2)
15. Maxwell's Silver Hammer (take 5)
16. Something (demo)
17. Come Together (take 1)
18. Come and Get It (demo)
19. Ain't She Sweet (EMI Studios, London, 24 July 1969)
20. Because (vocals only)
21. Let It Be (Apple Studios, London, 25 January 1969)
22. I Me Mine (take 16—1:47)
23. The End (composite mix)

CD: Paul McCartney, *Standing Stone* (EMI Classics CDC 5 56484–2), 1997[52]

1. Movement I: After heavy light years—Fire/rain. *Allegro energico*
2. Movement I: After heavy light years—Cell growth. *Semplice*
3. Movement I: After heavy light years—"Human" theme. (Maestoso)
4. Movement II: He awoke startled—Meditation. *Contemplativo*
5. Movement II: He awoke startled—Crystal ship. *Con moto scherzando*
6. Movement II: He awoke startled—Sea voyage. *Pulsating, with cool jazz feel*

7. Movement II: He awoke startled—Lost at sea. *Sognando*
8. Movement II: He awoke startled—Release. *Allegro con spirito*
9. Movement III: Subtle colours merged soft contours—Safe haven/standing stone. *Pastorale con moto*
10. Movement III: Subtle colours merged soft contours—Peaceful moment. *Andante tranquillo*
11. Movement III: Subtle colours merged soft contours—Messenger. *Energico*
12. Movement III: Subtle colours merged soft contours—Lament. *Lamentoso*
13. Movement III: Subtle colours merged soft contours—Trance. *Misterioso*
14. Movement III: Subtle colours merged soft contours—Eclipse. *Eroico*
15. Movement IV: Strings pluck, horns blow, drums beat—Glory tales. *Trionfale*
16. Movement IV: Strings pluck, horns blow, drums beat—Fugal celebration. *L'istesso tempo. Fresco*
17. Movement IV: Strings pluck, horns blow, drums beat—Rustic dance. *Rustico*
18. Movement IV: Strings pluck, horns blow, drums beat—Love duet. *Andante intimo*
19. Movement IV: Strings pluck, horns blow, drums beat—Celebration. *Andante*

CD: Paul McCartney, *Paul McCartney's Working Classical* (EMI Classical CDC 5 56897–2), 1999[53]

1. Junk
2. A Leaf
3. Haymakers
4. Midwife
5. Spiral
6. Warm and Beautiful
7. My Love
8. Maybe I'm Amazed
9. Calico Skies

10. Golden Earth Girl
11. Somedays
12. Tuesday
13. She's My Baby
14. The Lovely Linda

NOTES

1. Mark Lewisohn, *The Beatles' Recording Sessions* (New York: Harmony Books, 1988), 32.
2. Lewisohn, *Recording Sessions*, 37.
3. Lewisohn, *Recording Sessions*, 47.
4. Lewisohn, *Recording Sessions*, 53.
5. Lewisohn, *Recording Sessions*, 62.
6. Lewisohn, *Recording Sessions*, 69.
7. Lewisohn, *Recording Sessions*, 84.
8. Lewisohn, *Recording Sessions*, 114.
9. Lewisohn, *Recording Sessions*, 163.
10. Lewisohn, *Recording Sessions*, 164.
11. Lewisohn, *Recording Sessions*, 192.
12. Lewisohn, *Recording Sessions*, 199.
13. Lewisohn, *Recording Sessions*, 46.
14. Lewisohn, *Recording Sessions*, 131.
15. Lewisohn, *Recording Sessions*, 22.
16. Lewisohn, *Recording Sessions*, 24.
17. Lewisohn, *Recording Sessions*, 32.
18. Lewisohn, *Recording Sessions*, 35.
19. Lewisohn, *Recording Sessions*, 37.
20. Lewisohn, *Recording Sessions*, 43.
21. Lewisohn, *Recording Sessions*, 47.
22. Lewisohn, *Recording Sessions*, 52.
23. Lewisohn, *Recording Sessions*, 57.
24. Lewisohn, *Recording Sessions*, 60.
25. Lewisohn, *Recording Sessions*, 69.
26. Lewisohn, *Recording Sessions*, 83.
27. Lewisohn, *Recording Sessions*, 84.
28. Lewisohn, *Recording Sessions*, 98.
29. Lewisohn, *Recording Sessions*, 120–21.

30. Lewisohn, *Recording Sessions*, 131.

31. Lewisohn, *Recording Sessions*, 134.

32. Lewisohn, *Recording Sessions*, 152.

33. Lewisohn, *Recording Sessions*, 172.

34. Lewisohn, *Recording Sessions*, 177.

35. Lewisohn, *Recording Sessions*, 193.

36. Lewisohn, *Recording Sessions*, 196.

37. Joel Whitburn, *Top Pop Albums: 1955–2001* (Menomonee: Record Research Inc., 2001), 54.

37. Martin Strong, *The Great Rock Discography*, seventh ed. (Edinburgh: Canongate, 2004), 102.

39. Ian Peel, *The Unknown Paul McCartney: McCartney and the Avant-Garde* (London and Richmond, Surrey: Reynolds & Hearn, 2002), 231

40. Peel, *The Unknown Paul McCartney*, 232.

41. Peel, *The Unknown Paul McCartney*, 232.

42. Peel, *The Unknown Paul McCartney*, 232.

43. Whitburn, *Top Pop Albums*, 681.

44. Whitburn, *Top Pop Albums*, 430.

45. Peel, *The Unknown Paul McCartney*, 232.

46. Whitburn, *Top Pop Albums*, 563.

47. Paul McCartney, *Paul McCartney's Liverpool Oratorio*: Oratorio in eight movements, for soprano, mezzo-soprano, tenor, bass and boy treble soloists, boys' choir, SATB chorus and orchestra—vocal score. (London: Faber Music/MPL Communications), 1992.

48. Martin Strong, *The Great Rock Discography*, sixth ed. (Edinburgh: Canongate 2002), 896.

49. Peel, *The Unknown Paul McCartney*, 231.

50. Peel, *The Unknown Paul McCartney*, 232.

51. Peel, *The Unknown Paul McCartney*, 232.

52. Peel, *The Unknown Paul McCartney*, 233.

53. Peel, *The Unknown Paul McCartney*, 233.

BIBLIOGRAPHY

Adler, Samuel. *The Study of Orchestration*. New York: W.W. Norton, 1989.

Aldwell, Edward, and Carl Schachter. *Harmony and Voice-Leading*. San Diego: Harcourt, Brace, Jovanovich, 1989.

Babiuk, Andy. *The Beatles' Gear: All the Fab Four's Instruments from Stage to Studio*. San Francisco: Backbeat Books, 2001.

Beatles. *Anthology*. San Francisco: Chronicle Books, 2000.

——. *The Beatles Anthology*. DVD. Directed by Geoff Wonfor. London: Apple Corps Limited, 2003.

——. *The Beatles: Complete Scores*. London, New York, and Milwaukee, WI: Wise Publications, 1993.

——. *The Complete Beatles: Piano, Vocal, Guitar*. Winona, MN: H. Leonard, 1988.

——. *The Compleat Beatles*. VHS. Directed by Patrick Montgomery. New York: MGM/UA Home Video 1982.

Bernstein, Leonard. *The Unanswered Question: Six Talks at Harvard*. Cambridge, MA: Harvard University Press, 1976.

Brown, Peter. *The Love You Make: An Insider's Story of the Beatles*. New York: McGraw-Hill, 1983.

Cadwallader, Allen Clayton, and David Gagné. *Analysis of Tonal Music: A Schenkerian Approach*. New York: Oxford University Press, 1998.

Cook, David. A. *A History of Narrative Film*. New York: W.W. Norton, 1981.

Cook, Nicholas. *A Guide to Musical Analysis*. New York: G. Braziller, 1987.

Covach, John, and Graeme M. Boone, eds. *Understanding Rock: Essays in Musical Analysis.* New York: Oxford University Press, 1997.

Davies, Hunter. *The Beatles.* New York: W.W. Norton, 1978.

DiLello, Richard. *The Longest Cocktail Party: An Insider's Diary of the Beatles, Their Million-Dollar Apple Empire, and Its Wild Rise and Fall.* Ann Arbor, MI: Popular Culture, Inc., 1997.

Doggett, Peter. *Let It Be/Abbey Road: The Beatles.* New York and London: Schirmer Books/Prentice Hall International, 1998.

Dowlding, William J. *Beatlesongs.* New York: Simon & Schuster, 1989.

Droney, Maureen. *Mix Masters: Platinum Engineers Reveal Their Secrets for Success.* Boston: Berklee Press; Milwaukee: distributed by Hal Leonard, 2003.

Elliott, D. J. *Music Matters: A New Philosophy of Music Education.* New York: Oxford University Press, 1995.

Elliott, David. "On the Value of Music and Music Education." *Philosophy of Music Education Review* 1, no. 2 (Fall 1993): 81–93.

Everett, Walter. "The Beatles as Composers: The Genesis of *Abbey Road*, Side Two." Pp. 172–228 in *Concert Music, Rock, and Jazz since 1945: Essays and Analytical Studies*, ed. Elizabeth West Marvin and Richard Hermann. Rochester, NY: University of Rochester Press, 1995.

———. *The Beatles as Musicians:* Revolver *Through* The Anthology. New York: Oxford University Press, 1999.

———. *The Beatles as Musicians*: The Quarry Men *Through* Rubber Soul. New York: Oxford University Press, 2001

———. "Text Painting in the Foreground and Middleground of Paul McCartney's Beatle Song 'She's Leaving Home': A Musical Study of Psychological Conflict." *In Theory Only* (1987): 5–21.

Ferrara, Lawrence. "Phenomenology as a Tool for Musical Analysis." *The Musical Quarterly* 50 (1984): 355–73.

———. *Philosophy and the Analysis of Music.* New York: Greenwood Press, 1991.

Forte, Allen, and Steven Gilbert. *An Introduction to Schenkerian Analysis.* New York: Norton, 1982.

Frith, Simon. *Performing Rites: On the Value of Popular Music.* Oxford, UK: Oxford University Press, 1996.

Gambaccini, Paul. *The McCartney Interviews.* London: Omnibus, 1996

Gauldin, Robert. "Beethoven, Tristan, and the Beatles." *College Music Symposium* 30 (1990): 142–52.

Genette, Gerard. "Time and Narrative in *A la recherche du temps perdu*." Pp. 278–98 in *Essentials of the Theory of Fiction*, ed. Michael J. Hoffman and Patrick D. Murphy. Durham and London: Drake University Press, 1988.

Giuliano, Geoffrey. *Blackbird: The Life and Times of Paul McCartney*. New York: Plume, 1991.

Gopnik, Adam. "Carry That Weight." Review of Mark Hertsgaard, *A Day in the Life: The Music and Artistry of the Beatles*, and Ian MacDonald, *Revolution in the Head*. *The New Yorker* (1 May 1995).

Green, Douglass M. *Form in Tonal Music: An Introduction to Analysis*. New York: Holt, Rinehart and Winston, Inc., 1965.

Grout, Donald J., and Claude V. Palisca. *A History of Western Music*. New York: W.W. Norton, 2006.

Heinonen, Yrjö. *Beatlestudies*. Jyväskylä: University of Jyväskylä Dept. of Music, 1998.

Hertsgaard, Mark. *A Day in the Life: The Music and Artistry of the Beatles*. New York: Delacorte Press, 1995.

Ingarden, Roman. *The Literary Work of Art*. Evanston, IL: Northwestern University Press, 1973

Inglis, Ian, ed. *The Beatles, Popular Music, and Society: A Thousand Voices*. New York: St. Martin's Press, 2000.

Kennan, Kent, and Grantham, Donald. *The Technique of Orchestration*. Englewood Cliffs, NJ: Prentice Hall, 1990.

Kenney, William Howland. *Recorded Music in American Life: The Phonograph and Popular Memory, 1890–1945*. New York: Oxford University Press, 1999.

Kostka, Stefan M. *Materials and Techniques of Twentieth-Century Music*. Englewood Cliffs, NJ: Prentice Hall, 1990.

Kostka, Stefan M., and Dorothy Payne. *Tonal Harmony*. Boston: McGraw-Hill, 2000.

Kozinn, Allan. *The Beatles*. London: Phaidon, 1995.

Langer, Susanne, K. *Philosophy in a New Key: A Study in the Symbolism of Reason, Rite and Art*. Cambridge, MA: Harvard University Press, 1951.

———. *Feeling and Form: A Theory of Art*. New York: Scribner, 1953.

Larkin, Colin, ed., *The Encyclopedia of Popular Music, Third Edition, Volume Three*. London: Muze UK, 1998.

LaRue, Jan. *Guidelines for Style Analysis*. New York: W.W. Norton, 1970.

Lennon, John. *Lennon Remembers*. London; New York: Verso, 2000.

Lewisohn, Mark. *The Beatles' Recording Sessions*. New York: Harmony Books, 1988.

MacDonald, Ian. *Revolution in the Head: The Beatles' Records and the Sixties*. New York: H. Holt, 1994.

———. *Revolution in the Head: The Beatles' Records and the Sixties (Fully Updated Edition)*. London: Pimlico, 1998.

Manning, Peter. *Electronic and Computer Music*. New York: Oxford University Press, 2004.

Martin, George. *With a Little Help from My Friends: The Making of* Sgt. Pepper. Boston: Little, Brown, 1994.

Martin, George, and Jeremy Hornsby. *All You Need Is Ears.* New York: St. Martin's Press, 1979.

Martin, George, and William Pearson. *Summer of Love: The Making of* Sgt. Pepper. London: Macmillan, 1994.

Marvin, Elizabeth West, and Richard Hermann, eds. *Concert Music, Rock, and Jazz Since 1945: Essays and Analytical Studies.* Rochester, NY: University of Rochester Press, 1995.

McCartney, Paul. *Blackbird Singing: Poems and Lyrics, 1965–1999*, ed. Adrian Mitchell. New York: W.W. Norton, 2001.

———. Paul McCartney's Liverpool oratorio: oratorio in eight movements, for soprano, mezzo-soprano, tenor, bass and boy treble soloists, boys' choir, SATB chorus and orchestra—vocal score. London: Faber Music/MPL Communications, 1992.

———. *Wingspan/Text from Interviews with Paul McCartney*; text edited by Mark Lewisohn. Boston: Bulfinch, 2002.

Mellers, Wilfrid. *The Twilight of the Gods: The Music of the Beatles.* New York: Viking Press, 1973.

Meyer, Leonard B. *Emotion and Meaning in Music.* Chicago: University of Chicago Press, 1956.

———. *Explaining Music: Essays and Explorations.* Berkeley: University of California Press, 1973.

———. *Style and Music: Theory, History, and Ideology.* Philadelphia: University of Pennsylvania Press, 1989.

Miles, Barry, and Paul McCartney. *Many Years from Now.* New York: H. Holt, 1997.

Monaco, James. *How to Read a Film: The World of Movies, Media, and Multimedia, Language, History, Theory.* New York: Oxford University Press, 2000.

Moore, Allan F. *The Beatles:* Sgt. Pepper's Lonely Hearts Club Band. New York: Cambridge University Press, 1997.

Moorefield, Virgil Edwin. "From the Illusion of Reality to the Reality of Illusion: The Changing Role of the Producer in the Pop Recording Studio." Ph.D. diss., Princeton, NJ: Princeton University, 2001.

———. *The Producer as Composer: Shaping the Sounds of Popular Music.* Cambridge, MA: MIT Press, 2005.

Morgan, Robert P. *Twentieth-Century Music.* New York, London: W.W. Norton, 1991.

Norman, Philip. *Shout! The Beatles in Their Generation.* New York: Simon & Schuster, 1981.

O'Dell, Denis. *At the Apple's Core: The Beatles from the Inside.* London: Peter Owen Ltd., 2002.

O'Grady, Terence J. *The Beatles: A Musical Evolution.* Boston: Twayne Publishers, 1983.

Peel, Ian. *The Unknown Paul McCartney: McCartney and the Avant-Garde.* London and Richmond, Surrey: Reynolds & Hearn, 2002.

Phelps, Roger P., Lawrence Ferrara, and Thomas W. Goolsby. *A Guide to Research in Music Education,* 4th ed. Metuchen, NJ: Scarecrow Press, 1993.

Pohlmann, Ken C. *Principles of Digital Audio.* New York: McGraw Hill, 2000.

Pollock, Alan W. "Alan W. Pollock's Notes on . . . Series." Soundscapes.Info. 1999. http://www.icce.rug.nl/~soundscapes/DATABASES/AWP/awp-notes_on.shtml (July 15, 2007).

Riley, Tim. *Tell Me Why: A Beatles Commentary.* New York: Knopf/Random House, 1988.

Rosen, Charles. *The Frontiers of Meaning: Three Informal Lectures on Music.* New York: Hill and Wang, 1994.

———. *Sonata Forms.* New York and London: W.W. Norton, 1988.

———. *The Classical Style.* New York: W.W. Norton, 1997.

Rosenberg, Scott. "Peter Gabriel and Todd Rundgren Attempt to Interact with You." *Digital Culture.* 1994. http://www.wordyard.com/dmz/digicult/cdmusic -5-1-94.html (July 15, 2007).

Rowe, Robert. *Interactive Music Systems.* Cambridge, MA: MIT Press, 1993.

Russcol, Herbert. *An Introduction to Electronic Music.* New York: Prentice Hall, 1972.

Ryan, Kevin, and Brian Kehew. *Recording the Beatles: The Studio Equipment and Techniques Used to Create Their Classic Albums.* Houston: Curvebender Publishers, 2006.

Sadie, Stanley, ed. *The New Grove Dictionary of Music and Musicians, Second Edition, Volume Three.* New York: Thames & Hudson, 2001.

———. *Volume Six.* New York: Thames & Hudson, 2001.

———. *Volume Eight.* New York: Thames & Hudson, 2001.

———. *Volume Thirteen.* New York: Thames & Hudson, 2001.

———. *Volume Fifteen.* New York: Thames & Hudson, 2001.

———. *Volume Sixteen.* New York: Thames & Hudson, 2001.

———. *Volume Seventeen.* New York: Thames & Hudson, 2001.

———. *Volume Nineteen.* New York: Thames & Hudson, 2001.

Salzer, Felix. *Structural Hearing: Tonal Coherence in Music.* New York: Dover, 1982.

Sikov, Ed. *Mr. Strangelove: A Biography of Peter Sellers.* New York: Hyperion, 2002.

Spicer, Mark S. "British Pop-Rock Music in the Post-Beatles Era: Three Analytical Studies." Ph.D. diss., New Haven, CT: Yale University, 2001.

Strong, Martin. *The Great Rock Discography*, 6th ed. Edinburgh: Canongate, 2002.

Sullivan, Henry W. *The Beatles with Lacan: Rock 'n' roll as Requiem for the Modern Age*. New York: P. Lang, 1995.

Taylor, Alastair. *A Secret History*. London: Blake, 2001.

Terry, Carol D. *Here, There & Everywhere: The First International Beatles Bibliography, 1962–1982*. Ann Arbor, MI: Pierian Press, 1985.

Thomasson, Amie. "Roman Ingarden." *The Stanford Encyclopedia of Philosophy*. Spring 2004 edition. http://plato.stanford.edu/archives/spr2004/entries/ingarden/ (July. 15, 2007).

Thomson, Elizabeth, and David Gutman, eds. *The Lennon Companion: Twenty-five Years of Comment*. New York: Simon & Schuster/Macmillan, 1996.

Tovey, Donald Francis, Sir. *A Companion to Beethoven's Pianoforte Sonatas*. London: The Associated Board of the R. A. M. and R. C. M., 1931.

Wheelis, Allen. *The End of the Modern Age*. New York and London: Basic Books, 1971.

Whitburn, Joel. *Top Pop Albums: 1955–2001*. Menomonee, WI: Record Research Inc., 2001.

Wiener, Allen J. *The Beatles: A Recording History*. Jefferson: McFarland, 1986.

———. *The Beatles: The Ultimate Recording Guide*. Holbrook, MA: B. Adams, 1994.

INDEX

ABOUT THE AUTHOR

THOMAS MACFARLANE completed his Ph.D. in music composition at New York University, where he teaches courses in music theory and composition. He also coteaches a course in the performing arts in Western civilization with the chair of the NYU Department of Music and Performing Arts Professions, Dr. Lawrence Ferrara. As a composer, MacFarlane has had works performed at venues in Italy, Hungary, Romania, and the United States. His original score for the film "The Sweetest Sound" premiered in May 2001 at Lincoln Center, and his orchestral composition "Suite for Mingus" was performed and recorded at Merkin Hall on November 5, 2003.

In February 2005 he collaborated with Dr. John Gilbert on music and sound design for "Provocative Acts," an original presentation by the NYU Program in Educational Theatre. In April 2005 he was a composer and musician for "Lubricious Transfer," a live Internet collaboration between artists at New York University and the University of California at Santa Cruz. In 1997 he released a CD of original works, *Longtime*, which was structured as an essay on the development of recording technique. The production of this album employed a wide variety of formats—from 78rpm sources to analog and digital multitrack—in an effort to raise pertinent questions regarding the existence of paradigmatic shifts in the process of music composition.